THE MACY'S CULINARY COUNCIL

# THANKSGIVING & HOLIDAY

## COOKBOOK

# THE MACY'S CULINARY COUNCIL
# THANKSGIVING & HOLIDAY
## COOKBOOK

RECIPES BY

### The Macy's Culinary Council

FOREWORD BY

### Terry J. Lundgren

Editorial direction and text by STEVE SIEGELMAN

Art direction by CATHERINE JACOBES

Food photography by MAREN CARUSO

Style direction by GEORGE DOLESE

**BOOK KITCHEN**
San Francisco

# CONTENTS

# Foreword

MACY'S THANKSGIVING DAY PARADE is celebrating its 85th Anniversary. For many generations, watching the Macy's Parade has become the opening ritual for millions of families on this uniquely American holiday.

In fact, the Parade has become synonymous with the holiday itself. Many fans simply refer to it as "The Macy's Day Parade."

There have been many books published by and about Macy's over the years, but this one is unique. In these pages, Macy's own Culinary Council, a group of cooking superstars, joins with the Macy's Parade Group to make this very special holiday a *total* experience. In short, this is the book that puts "Thanksgiving" front and center in the "The Macy's Day Parade."

Just as Macy's Parade represents the official kickoff of the holiday season, this new cookbook features ideas for Thanksgiving Day as well as recipes and approaches for celebrating all the key moments of an American holiday season that is special in its diversity and multicultural flavor. Chefs Emeril Lagasse, Tom Douglas, Marc Forgione and Cat Cora present their own Thanksgiving menus. Nancy Silverton teaches us how to make-over our leftovers Wolfgang Puck and Tim Scott entice us with brunch and buffet ideas. Todd English does his take on the Feast of Seven Fishes. Rick Bayless prepares a joyous Christmas dinner, while Michelle Bernstein celebrates Hanukkah. Marcus Samuelsson presents an All-American Julbord (think "yule" plus "smorgasbord"), Ming Tsai introduces a Dumpling Party and Takashi Yagihashi celebrates the New Year without dropping the ball.

This is a book about holiday cooking, but like the Parade, it represents so much more . . . both are imaginative recipes for bringing people together with families and friends for Thanksgiving and throughout the holidays.

From the Macy's family to yours, wishing you Happy Holidays and a season of good eating!

Terry J. Lundgren
Chairman, President and CEO of Macy's, Inc.

# AMERICA'S FAVORITE PARADE

It's more than a spectacle. It's a beloved national tradition. As the aroma of roasting turkey fills the air in homes all across America, millions of families and friends sit down together to enjoy the magic of the Macy's Thanksgiving Day Parade.

So, where did this great American institution come from, and how does it come together year after year?

"A lot of people think we dust off the balloons and floats a few days before Thanksgiving, and we're ready to go," says parade Executive Producer Amy Kule. "But it's actually a year-round effort by hundreds—ultimately thousands—of Macy's employees that's entirely produced by our own artists and craftspeople. And the Monday after Thanksgiving, we're all back at work, ready to start in on next year's parade."

It's been a homegrown affair ever since it began in 1924, when a group of Macy's employees, mostly immigrants and first-generation Americans, gathered on the corner of 145th Street and Convent Avenue in New York City. It was Thanksgiving Day, and this was their Christmas party—and their chance to give thanks to America. What they couldn't have known was that they were creating one of the nation's most enduring and best-loved holiday celebrations.

"It's pretty amazing to be part of that tradition almost a century later," says Amy Kule. "That same spirit, gratitude, and awe still permeates everything we do. And just like those who came before us, we know it's our job to pass this iconic event on to the next generation."

# 1924
## A GREAT AMERICAN TRADITION BEGINS

For its first decade, although held on Thanksgiving, the parade was known as Macy's Christmas Parade. Here, staffers escort the giant Macy's tree through Manhattan.

# LET'S HAVE A PARADE!

At the height of the Roaring Twenties, Macy's on Herald Square was the largest store on earth. And as Thanksgiving 1924 approached, everyone at Macy's agreed—it was time to celebrate.

"Let's have a parade!" someone suggested. And so, dressed in costumes, with fanciful horse-drawn floats and live animals borrowed from the Central Park Zoo, a thousand Macy's staffers frolicked through six miles of Manhattan—from Harlem to Macy's on Herald Square—to the delight of nearly a million spectators. There were clowns and jugglers, stilt-walkers and marching bands, and, of course, at the tail end of the parade, Santa himself, ushering in the start of the holiday season. The exuberant spirit of the men and women of Macy's had created a celebration that would become world famous.

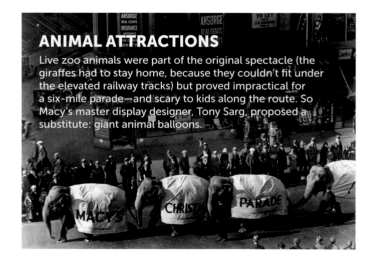

## ANIMAL ATTRACTIONS

Live zoo animals were part of the original spectacle (the giraffes had to stay home, because they couldn't fit under the elevated railway tracks) but proved impractical for a six-mile parade—and scary to kids along the route. So Macy's master display designer, Tony Sarg, proposed a substitute: giant animal balloons.

## 1927
### BRING ON THE BALLOONS

Designer Tony Sarg, who was also a master puppeteer, enlisted the Goodyear Company to produce giant rubber balloons, which he and his staff joined together and painted to create fantastical animals. Thanks to his inspired idea, balloon characters have been a signature of the parade ever since.

### BALLOONATICS

Sarg's first balloons were filled with air, not helium, so they had to be held aloft on long poles. He thought of these first balloons as upside-down marionettes, and called them "balloonatics."

## 1929
### REWARD IF FOUND

With the freed balloons floating as far away as 100 miles from the city, retrieving them was a challenge. Macy's put a return address label on each balloon promising a $100 reward. But this created a hunting frenzy, as "poachers" started shooting the balloons down out of the sky, and aviators even began attempting to lasso them in midair.

## 1928
### BIG BANG!

In 1928, Sarg filled his balloons with helium so they could float high above the crowd. At the end of the parade, each balloon was dramatically released into the air. But the finale was a bust! No one had realized that the helium would expand, causing the balloons to burst. By the following year, pressure valves had been installed to fix the problem.

# 1933
## GROUNDED!

When a pilot had a close call with a cat balloon, the balloons were grounded forever. Now they're carefully deflated at the end of the parade route and brought back to the studio for storage.

# 1934
## THE MAGIC OF MICKEY

Macy's collaboration with the Walt Disney Company on the Mickey Mouse balloon was the first of many media partnerships that would bring icons of popular culture to life, from Snoopy and Kermit to Buzz Lightyear and Dora the Explorer.

# 1942
## THE WAR YEARS

From 1942 to 1944, World War II brought the parade to a halt for the first and only time in its history. With rubber and helium in short supply, the balloons were donated to provide 650 pounds of scrap rubber for the war effort.

# 1946
## READY FOR PRIME TIME

The parade was broadcast locally for the first time in 1946 and nationally in 1947, transforming it from a New York tradition to a national institution.

# 1947
## MIRACLE ON 34TH STREET

The classic film *Miracle on 34th Street* put the parade on the map for audiences worldwide. It opened in May, and miraculously was so popular it was still playing to packed houses at Thanksgiving.

# 1958
## THE ROCKETTES STEP IN

For more than half a century, the Radio City Rockettes® have brought their sparkling glamour and high-kicking precision to the parade.

# 1966
## A NEW ERA OF CREATIVITY

In 1960, Macy's hired renowned designer Manfred "Manny" Bass to build the parade's magical floats. In 1966, Bass opened the Macy's Parade Studio, a workshop for constructing a new generation of "theater in the round" floats. His endless imagination and creative vision defined the look of the parade for 40 years.

# 1970s
## BEST OF BROADWAY

The parade has been called "the longest running show on Broadway," and ever since the 1970s, cast members from the hottest New York musicals have been featured. Here, Constance Towers stars in a number from *The King and I*.

# 1979
## BALLOONS IN THE HOUSE

When Goodyear decided to get out of the balloon-making business, the parade team said, "we can do this!" Ever since, the balloons have been designed by the Macy's Parade Studio.

# MAKING THE MAGIC

It was a foundry, and then, for years, a Tootsie Roll factory. But since the 1960s, this massive warehouse in Hoboken, New Jersey, has been the Macy's Parade Studio, where designers and craftsmen make all of the parade's floats and balloons by hand.

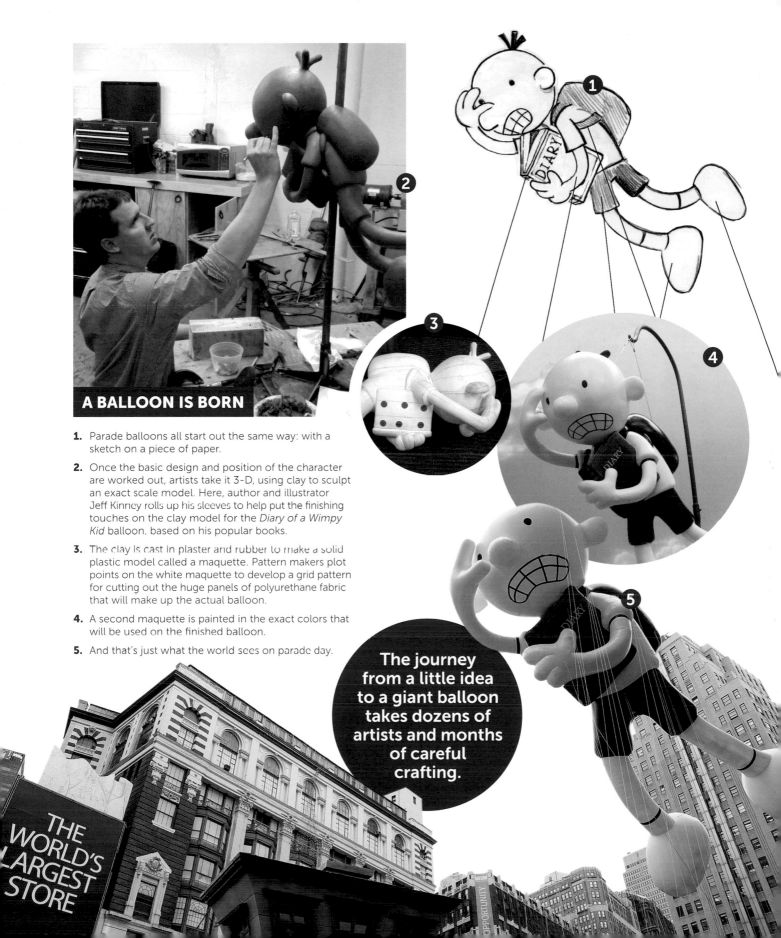

## A BALLOON IS BORN

1. Parade balloons all start out the same way: with a sketch on a piece of paper.

2. Once the basic design and position of the character are worked out, artists take it 3-D, using clay to sculpt an exact scale model. Here, author and illustrator Jeff Kinney rolls up his sleeves to help put the finishing touches on the clay model for the *Diary of a Wimpy Kid* balloon, based on his popular books.

3. The clay is cast in plaster and rubber to make a solid plastic model called a maquette. Pattern makers plot points on the white maquette to develop a grid pattern for cutting out the huge panels of polyurethane fabric that will make up the actual balloon.

4. A second maquette is painted in the exact colors that will be used on the finished balloon.

5. And that's just what the world sees on parade day.

The journey from a little idea to a giant balloon takes dozens of artists and months of careful crafting.

THE WORLD'S LARGEST STORE

# RECIPE FOR A PARADE

## Serves about 54 million

2,400 marching musicians
1,600 balloon handlers
3.5 million live spectators
50 million TV viewers
27 floats
Dozens of push floats
50 balloons
400,000 cubic feet of helium
250 lbs. of confetti
3,500 costumes
4,000 volunteers
385 kids
1,600 cheerleaders
24 Rockettes
850 clowns
1 Santa

Start planning a year in advance. As Thanksgiving Day approaches, assemble all ingredients. Twenty-four hours ahead of time, start the final preparation process. Serve immediately, rain or shine. Repeat annually.

## 2,400 MARCHING MUSICIANS

Two years in advance of each parade, Macy's receives hundreds of audition tapes from high school, college, and professional bands. The best of them, some up to 300 strong, make the trip to New York for the experience of a lifetime.

## 850 CLOWNS

The parade clowns are mostly Macy's employees who love the fun of entertaining—and helping out with crowd control.

## 27 FLOATS

## 400,000 CUBIC FEET OF HELIUM

It takes a lot of helium to make Macy's famous parade balloons larger-than-life.

## 3.5 MILLION LIVE SPECTATORS

## 50 BALLOONS

## 3,500 COSTUMES

The night before the parade, eight massive trucks arrive at a midtown hotel where Macy's costume operation sets up shop in a series of ballrooms. Within two hours, starting at 5:00 a.m., 3,500 performers get in costume and makeup, then board buses heading uptown to the parade's starting point.

# 24-HOUR COUNTDOWN

During those final 24 hours before Thanksgiving, while you're polishing the silverware, pulling out the turkey platter, and getting the meal together, 4,000 volunteers, some of whom fly in just for the occasion, are racing to put the finishing touches on the parade. From Hoboken to the Upper West Side, it's a mad dash to the starting line for parade organizers.

## WEDNESDAY, NOON

### BALLOON INFLATION

For nearly a million people who line Central Park West, the day-before spectacle of balloon inflation is a must-see event. It takes about an hour and a half to fill each balloon—and four trailer trucks of helium! Depending on the balloon, the feet might be filled with a mix of helium and air, so they float lower than the head.

## 10:00 P.M.

### MANY HANDS MAKE LIGHTS MOVE

In an eight-hour process that takes place all along the streets of the parade route, a team of technicians repositions hundreds of specially designed New York lampposts and traffic signals so they are parallel to the curb to make room for the passing balloons and floats.

## MIDNIGHT

### THROUGH THE LINCOLN TUNNEL

To make the journey from Hoboken to Manhattan, the entire parade has to pass through the eye of a very small needle: the Lincoln Tunnel. The massive floats, each a miniature theater, must be carefully designed to fold up and break down to no more than 8' wide and 12' 6" high to squeeze through the tunnel.

## THURSDAY, 1:00 A.M.

### FLOAT ASSEMBLY

The convoy of floats arrives on Central Park West and lines up in the exact parade order. Working fast in the dark of night, the overnight crew puts the floats together, testing to make sure they're properly and safely assembled with all of their animation working perfectly.

# 3:00 A.M.

## REHEARSAL ON 34TH STREET

The bands and show numbers do a fully costumed dress rehearsal for the television cameras. Every move is choreographed and timed to the second to make the telecast clock in at exactly three hours.

# 9:00 A.M.

## IT'S SHOWTIME!

With the traditional words, "Let's have a parade!" and the official ribbon cutting, the festivities begin at the stroke of 9:00 a.m.

# NOON

## HERE COMES SANTA CLAUS

As they pass in front of Macy's, Santa and his reindeer always mark the end of the parade—and the official start of the holiday season.

# 5:00 P.M.

## PACK IT UP

As soon as the floats and balloons arrive at the end point, they are quickly dismantled or deflated and packed up for the journey home. By late afternoon, the entire show is neatly stored at the Parade Studio for next year.

# THE PARADE FAMILY

Each year, a family of more than 4,000 volunteers—including thousands of Macy's employees and their friends and families, along with die-hard parade enthusiasts from all over the U.S.—descend on New York for a very different kind of Thanksgiving experience. They celebrate the holiday by giving the world its favorite parade.

## WATCH THE PILOT

Kathy Kramer (center, in green cap), a longtime balloon pilot and Macy's Director of Lease Administration, poses with the Ronald McDonald crew. Her directions guide this team of more than 50 handlers safely and in perfect step through the streets of New York.

## THE VOICE

Scott Byers, Director of Event Administration with the Parade and Entertainment Group and the company's official historian, is also the "uptown voice" of the parade, introducing each parade element into the line of march over the PA system for the crowds to hear at the starting line.

## BALLOON HANDLERS

Each balloon is guided through the streets by as many as 100 trained and precisely organized handlers, captains, and pilots. Equal parts puppeteers and safety technicians, they make constant adjustments in line tension, position, and height, navigating winds and avoiding obstacles to keep the spectators safe and the balloons in peak performance.

## THE DREAM TEAM

The creative and logistical gurus behind the parade (left to right): Bill Schermerhorn (VP, Creative Director), John Piper (VP, Macy's Parade Studio), Robin Hall (Senior VP, Macy's Parade and Entertainment Group), Susan Babb (VP, Event Operations), Jordan Dabby (VP, Partnership Marketing), and Amy Kule (Executive Producer, Group VP, Macy's Parade and Entertainment Group).

## LEGACY VOLUNTEERS

Talk about dedication! Roy Kovats, Elsie Angiono, Roseann Levy, and Bob Grant have each volunteered to work at the parade for more than 50 years.

## MACY'S CLOWN U

Those 850 men, women, and kids in greasepaint, wild costumes, and crazy wigs aren't just clowning around. These volunteers, mostly Macy's employees and their families, go through Macy's Clown U, an intensive training program led by clown instructors from the Big Apple Circus.

# THANKSGIVING FRIDAY

When you work on the parade, you're in it for 24 hours or more, and that means skipping Thanksgiving dinner altogether. But Macy's has a creative solution: a fabulous day-after feast that's very much a family affair.

It's a traditional Thanksgiving dinner for 200 parade staffers and their families on Black Friday, right in the Macy's Parade Studio. Starting the night before, Eugene Flynn, the owner of Amanda's, a popular Hoboken restaurant, and a team of his chefs and waiters transform the studio into a banquet hall, with linen-topped tables and holiday decorations.

There are drinks and nibbles, followed by a salad course, a lavish buffet with turkey and every imaginable side dish, and a lineup of favorite desserts. "For those of us who live and breathe the parade, this is our family, and this is our Thanksgiving dinner," says Parade Studio VP, John Piper. "We wouldn't have it any other way."

Here are two favorite recipes from Macy's Black Friday family Thanksgiving dinner. "We get requests for these every year," says Eugene Flynn. "I wouldn't dare take them off the menu, and I hope they find a place on your Thanksgiving menu, too."

### Brussels Sprouts with Applewood Smoked Bacon

SERVES 8

8 ounces thick-sliced applewood smoked bacon, cut crosswise into ¼-inch-wide strips

½ cup minced onions

2 cloves garlic, minced

½ cup white wine

2 pounds Brussels sprouts, ends and tough outer leaves removed

5 cups chicken or vegetable broth

Kosher salt and freshly ground pepper

Cook the bacon in a large sauté pan over medium-high heat until it has rendered its fat and is crisp, 8 to 10 minutes.

Pour off all but 2 tablespoons of the rendered fat and reserve for another use. Remove half the bacon to be used as garnish and set on a paper towel–lined plate to drain. Add the onions and garlic to the pan. Sauté until softened but not browned, 5 to 7 minutes.

Add the wine, raise the heat to high, and bring to a boil, stirring with a wooden spoon to scrape up any bacon bits stuck to the bottom of the pan. Cook for about 6 minutes, until the wine is reduced to a thick syrup.

Add the Brussels sprouts and the broth, bring to a boil, and cook until the sprouts are easily pierced with a knife, 12 to 15 minutes. Using a slotted spoon, transfer the sprouts to a serving dish.

Over high heat, reduce the cooking liquid in the pan until it is thick and syruplike, about 5 minutes. Pour the reduced cooking liquid over the sprouts and toss to coat them evenly.

Taste and adjust seasoning with salt and pepper if desired. Sprinkle the reserved bacon over the top and serve.

### Blue Cheese Potatoes au Gratin

SERVES 8 TO 10

2 tablespoons butter

1 quart heavy cream

3 pounds Idaho russet potatoes, peeled and sliced ⅛ inch thick (preferably on a mandoline)

2 teaspoons kosher salt

5 ounces Maytag blue cheese, crumbled

Kosher salt

Ground white pepper

Preheat the oven to 350°F. Butter a 9-by-12-inch baking dish.

Pour the cream into a large, heavy-bottomed pot over medium heat and slowly bring to a boil, watching carefully so the cream does not boil over. As soon as the cream reaches a boil, add the sliced potatoes and salt and stir to combine. Bring the mixture back to a simmer (stirring often so the potatoes don't stick to the bottom) and cook until the mixture has thickened and the potatoes are almost fully cooked, about 10 minutes. Remove from the heat.

Layer one-third of the potatoes in the bottom of the prepared baking dish. Sprinkle one-third of the blue cheese evenly over the potatoes and season with a little salt and white pepper. Repeat the layers twice, ending with the blue cheese. Pour any cream left in the pan over the potatoes, and cover the dish loosely with foil.

Bake until the potatoes are cooked through, about 45 minutes. Remove the foil and continue to bake until the top is browned and lightly crusted, about 15 minutes more. Let rest for 10 minutes before serving.

### PILGRIM AT HEART

For more than a decade, Eugene Flynn has made sure the Macy's parade staff is rewarded with a great Thanksgiving dinner. "We really put our heart and soul into it," he says, "because Thanksgiving is my favorite holiday—and I really love the parade." In fact, he and his family love it so much, they get up at 4:30 on Thanksgiving morning to be in it! He's been everything from a clown to a doodlebug driver. "I always wanted to be that one lucky pilgrim who rides on the turkey float," he says, "and last year my dream came true…sort of. They re-created the parade for the movie *Tower Heist*, and I got to be the pilgrim!"

# MEET THE CHEFS

The Macy's Culinary Council is a dream team of 13 star chefs from across America. This book is their holiday celebration for you—a chance to share the flavors and traditions that make the season magical for them and the people they love.

**RICK BAYLESS** is the owner of Chicago restaurants Frontera Grill, Topolobampo, XOCO, and Tortas Frontera at O'Hare Airport, as well as Frontera Fresco, his upscale, quick-service concept at Macy's State Street, Old Orchard, and Union Square. More recently, Rick took on consulting-chef responsibilities at the new Red O in LA. Rick was awarded 1995 Chef of the Year by the International Association of Culinary Professionals, 1998 Humanitarian of the Year by the James Beard Foundation, and 2002 Cooking Teacher of the Year by *Bon Appétit*. In 2007, Frontera Grill was named America's Outstanding Restaurant of the Year by the James Beard Foundation. In 2009, Rick Bayless was crowned *Top Chef Master* on the Bravo network. Rick hosts *Mexico: One Plate at a Time* on public television, now in its eighth season, and just recently released his newest cookbook, *Fiesta at Rick's*.

**MICHELLE BERNSTEIN** is a Miami native of Jewish and Latin descent. Since the pivotal Mango Gang era in the late '80s and early '90s, virtually no other Miami chef has made as big a splash on the national culinary scene. This passionate culinarian has dazzled diners and critics alike with her sublime cuisine and a personality as bright and vibrant as the Florida sun. "My food is luxurious but approachable," says Bernstein, a James Beard Award winner (Best Chef South 2008) and author of *Cuisine a Latina* (Houghton Mifflin Harcourt, 2008). "You don't need heavy-handed technique and over-the-top presentations to make a dish work. It's about amazing ingredients, layered flavors, and simplicity. I cook the food I love, and I think that love translates to the diners." Right now, diners are loving Bernstein's cuisine at her three successful Miami outposts, Michy's, Sra. Martinez, and Crumb on Parchment, which she owns and operates with her partner/husband David Martinez. Sporting distinctly different styles and cuisines, all three display the earnestness, passion, and dedication that have made Bernstein one of the region's brightest culinary stars. In addition to an ever-growing restaurant empire—Michelle Bernstein at The Omphoy in Palm Beach, Florida, opened fall 2009—Bernstein recently launched the Miami chapter of Common Threads, an after-school program dedicated to teaching underprivileged kids ages 8 to 11 to cook, socialize, and eat healthy.

**CAT CORA** made television history in 2005 by becoming the first and only female Iron Chef on Food Network's *Iron Chef America*. The mother of four boys has authored three top-selling cookbooks; has opened three restaurants in partnerships with Macy's (CCQ), Walt Disney World Boardwalk Resort (Kouzzina by Cat Cora), and her newest venture, Cat Cora's Kitchen, which debuted in the »

TOP ROW, LEFT TO RIGHT: Emeril Lagasse, Marcus Samuelsson, Ming Tsai, Todd English, Tom Douglas, Nancy Silverton, Cat Cora, Tim Scott. BOTTOM ROW, LEFT TO RIGHT: Michelle Bernstein, Marc Forgione, Rick Bayless, Takashi Yagihashi, Wolfgang Puck.

new Virgin Terminal 2 at San Francisco International in April 2011; and has launched her own collection of wines, Coranation. In January 2011, Cora introduced her first line of cookware with Starfrit, Canada's leading purveyor of eco-friendly cookware and kitchen gadgets, and introduced her Cat Cora's Kitchen line of olive oils, vinegar, cooking sauces, and tapenades by Gaea, the leader in Greek specialty food products. Cora released her first children's book, *Suitcase Surprise for Mommy* (Dial Books, 2011) a sweet and comforting tool for kids and parents to use when mom or dad have to travel, in March of 2011. Cora is the cohost of Disney's *Muppets Kitchen with Cat Cora* and *Hasty Tasty* Web series. She is currently working on a project with the Oprah Winfrey Network (OWN) and is a contributing food and lifestyle editor for *O, The Oprah Magazine*. In 2004, Cora, an avid philanthropist and UNICEF spokesperson, founded Chefs for Humanity in response to the tsunami disaster in Indonesia. This not-for-profit organization has partnered with Share Our Strength and the World Food Programme to provide nutrition education and hunger relief worldwide. For more information, please visit www.catcora.com and follow Cat on Twitter (@catcora) and Facebook.

**TOM DOUGLAS,** along with his wife and business partner, Jackie Cross, owns ten of Seattle's most exciting restaurants: Dahlia Lounge, Etta's, Palace Kitchen, Lola, Serious Pie (with two locations), Seatown Snack Bar, Cuoco, Ting Momo, and Brave Horse Tavern. With almost 30 years in the biz, Tom helped put Seattle on the culinary map by cooking global cuisine using regional and seasonal ingredients. Tom also runs a retail bakery, Dahlia Bakery, now with a second counter, the Dahlia Workshop, a catering business, Tom Douglas's Catering and Events, and an event space, Palace Ballroom. All of Tom's restaurants are located in the downtown Seattle and South Lake Union neighborhood. Tom is the author of three cookbooks, *Tom Douglas' Seattle Kitchen* (Morrow, 2001), *Tom's Big Dinners* (Morrow, 2003), and *I Love Crab Cakes!* (Morrow, 2006), with one more in the works. In addition, Tom's specialty food line, which includes Rub with Love spice rubs and barbecue and teriyaki sauces, is sold nationwide. His line of Tom Douglas by Pinzon kitchen tools is sold in partnership with Amazon.com.

**TODD ENGLISH** is a renowned chef, restaurateur, author, entrepreneur, and television star based in Boston, Massachusetts, and New York City. In 1989, English opened his first restaurant, Olives, in Charlestown, Massachusetts, which quickly drew national and international applause for English's interpretive rustic Mediterranean cuisine. In recent years, English has established Olives as one of the most prestigious names in the nation by opening locations in New York and Las Vegas. He is a four-time James Beard Award winner and inductee into the James Beard Foundation's Who's Who in Food and Beverage in America. English has published three critically acclaimed cookbooks; created the record-breaking housewares line, The Todd English Collection; and hosts the Emmy-nominated PBS travel series *Food Trip with Todd English*. Todd English Enterprises includes over twenty innovative restaurants spanning the country. Most recently, Todd opened the Todd English P.U.B. at Las Vegas's City Center, as well as two new restaurants in New York City, his European-inspired Plaza Food Hall by Todd English at the iconic Plaza Hotel, and his French-inspired Brasserie Ça Va, located in the heart of the theater district. Todd opened his first dessert concept, Isabelle's CurlyCakes, with his 17-year-old daughter, Isabelle, in her hometown of Boston, Massachusetts. Todd English is also very involved with several local and national charities, including Citymeals-on-Wheels, Share Our Strength, Men with Heart, the Boys and Girls Clubs, Volunteers of America, Autism Speaks, and City Harvest.

**MARC FORGIONE,** winner of season three of *The Next Iron Chef,* is the chef/owner of Restaurant Marc Forgione in New York City. Recognized with a glowing two-star review from Sam Sifton of the *New York Times*, Restaurant Marc Forgione is an approachable place "that people walk by and are compelled to enter and where the ingredients are the star." In addition to the Iron Chef title, Forgione was most recently awarded his second Michelin star in the 2011 guide, making him the youngest American-born chef and owner to receive the honor in consecutive years (2010, 2011).

**EMERIL LAGASSE** is the chef/proprietor of 12 award-winning restaurants in New Orleans, Las Vegas, Orlando, and Bethlehem, PA. He is a national TV personality, who has hosted over 2,000 shows on the Food Network and is the food correspondent for ABC's *Good Morning America* in addition to shows airing on the Cooking Channel and the Hallmark Channel. Emeril is the best-selling author of 16 cookbooks, most recently releasing *Sizzling Skillets and Other One-Pot Wonders*. He joined the Martha Stewart family of brands in 2008; Martha Stewart Living Omnimedia (NYSE: MSO) acquired the assets related to Emeril's media and merchandising business, including television programming, cookbooks, and the emerils.com website and his licensed kitchen and food products. In September 2002, Emeril established the Emeril Lagasse Foundation to support and encourage culinary arts and education programs for children. Lagasse's restaurant company, Emeril's Homebase, is located in New Orleans and houses restaurant operations, a culinary test kitchen, and a boutique store for his signature products.

**WOLFGANG PUCK** is known the world over for creating incomparable tastes and service rivaled by none. His legendary name carries an undeniable cachet, synonymous with a bold, innovative school of cooking that redefined fine dining in America and around the world. His trademark dishes, coupled with his unmistakable panache and passion, have revolutionized the culinary industry. Wolfgang Puck is the original celebrity chef, whose empire has flourished for decades with its proven formula of exceptional and consistent cuisine, service, management, and design. The master chef and restaurateur has carefully crafted a vast empire since the early 1980s which includes 18 fine dining restaurants, premium catering services, more than 80 fast-casual operations, and food and product merchandise divided into three companies, the Wolfgang Puck Fine Dining Group, Wolfgang Puck Catering, and Wolfgang Puck Worldwide, Inc.

**MARCUS SAMUELSSON** is an award-winning, internationally acclaimed chef, restaurateur, and cookbook author who has thrilled the food scene with a blend of culture and artistic excellence. Among his many accolades, chef Samuelsson holds the record for being the youngest person ever to receive two impressive three-star ratings from the *New York Times*. He is the author of three award-winning cookbooks: *Aquavit and the New Scandinavian Cuisine, The Soul of a New Cuisine,* and *New American Table.* Chef Samuelsson has been honored by the prestigious James Beard Foundation on multiple occasions, including Rising Star Chef (1999), Best Chef: New York City (2003), and Best International Cookbook (2007); and he continues to bring humility to the art of food and his UNICEF endeavors, working toward immunization and curbing malnutrition for children throughout the world. In November 2009, chef Samuelsson was selected to cook the Obama Administration's first state dinner, and the following year, he beat out twenty-one fellow chefs on the second season of the hit Bravo series *Top Chef Masters,* winning $115,000 for the UNICEF Tap Project. Chef Samuelsson opened his latest New York City restaurant, Red Rooster Harlem, in December 2010; and in 2011, he cofounded FoodRepublic.com, the first food and lifestyle website for men. He is a judge on Food Network's *Chopped* and *24 Hour Restaurant Battle,* and has appeared on numerous media platforms, including the *Today Show, Late Night with Jimmy Fallon,* and *The Martha Stewart Show.*

**TIM SCOTT** is the corporate executive chef for Macy's North and is responsible for creating recipes and menus for 20 full-service restaurants and 45 other fresh food operations throughout the country. With the expansion of the Macy's Foods Division, he is also currently working on integrating fresh-food concepts nationwide. He frequently teaches cooking classes for both adults and children. Tim started cooking professionally at the age of 14 and is a graduate of the Culinary Institute of America.

**NANCY SILVERTON** is an award-winning pastry chef and the founder of La Brea Bakery and co-owner of Mozza in Los Angeles and Singapore. Her cookbooks, *Nancy Silverton's Pastries from the La Brea Bakery* and *Nancy Silverton's Breads from the La Brea Bakery,* were nominated for awards from Julia Child and the James Beard Foundation, respectively. Silverton's eighth book, *The Mozza Cookbook,* was released in August 2011.

**MING TSAI** opened Blue Ginger in February 1998, and ever since, the East-West bistro and its chef have been honored with numerous accolades, including the James Beard Award for the 2002 Best Chef Northeast. Blue Ginger has been rated among the top five most popular restaurants in Boston by the *Zagat Restaurant Guide* for the last ten years. In 2008, Blue Ginger expanded, creating three private dining rooms and the Lounge at Blue Ginger, serving an Asian tapas menu featuring Ming's Bings. Ming, an Emmy Award winner, currently hosts and is executive producer of the Emmy-nominated public television cooking show *Simply Ming,* currently in its ninth season. In addition, he hosts a weekly vodcast offering tips and tutorials on everything from filleting fish to decanting wine. Ming is the author of four cookbooks: *Blue Ginger, Simply Ming, Ming's Master Recipes,* and his 2010 release, *Simply Ming One-Pot Meals.* Ming is a national spokesperson for FAAN (Food Allergy and Anaphylaxis Network).

**TAKASHI YAGIHASHI** opened his Chicago eatery, Takashi Restaurant, in December 2007. The restaurant received widespread praise in its first year. Both *Esquire* and *Chicago* magazine named Takashi the Best New Restaurant of 2008. Zagat rated the restaurant 29 for food, the best rating in Chicago. Takashi earned a one-star rating in *The Michelin Guide Chicago 2010,* one of only 18 restaurants to do so. Takashi also operates Noodles by Takashi Yagihashi, a rustic Japanese noodle restaurant that opened in 2006 at Macy's on State Street in Chicago. He has run such famed kitchens as Okada at the Wynn Hotel in Las Vegas and Tribute in Detroit. In 2003, he was named Best Chef in the Midwest, by the James Beard Foundation. In 2000, Takashi graced the cover of *Food and Wine* as one of America's Ten Best New Chefs. His first cookbook, *Takashi's Noodles,* was released April 2009. His newest restaurant, Slurping Turtle, a Japanese tapas and noodle bar, opened in summer 2011.

# THANKSGIVING

# THANKSGIVING BASICS

Once you master the classic Thanksgiving favorites, you can begin adding your own creative twists and touches, like our chefs have done throughout this book. To get you started, here's a hit parade of easy, made-from-scratch holiday recipes from the Macy's kitchens—from perfect turkey and gravy to all the traditional trimmings.

# Chef's Mix

Here's the famous party mix, updated with a few contemporary chef's surprises. It's a year-round crowd-pleaser that goes with everything from milk to martinis.

**MAKES ABOUT 14 CUPS**

2 cups wheat cereal squares

2 cups rice cereal squares

2 cups corn cereal squares

1 cup oat cereal "O"s

3 cups corn snacks (such as Bugles)

1 cup cheese cracker squares

1 cup pretzel sticks

1 cup Marcona almonds or smoked almonds

1 cup salted, roasted pumpkin seeds

4 tablespoons butter

¼ cup extra virgin olive oil

2 tablespoons Worcestershire sauce

¾ teaspoon onion powder

1 teaspoon garlic powder

2 teaspoons hot smoked paprika

1 teaspoon dried orange peel

½ teaspoon dried sage, rubbed between fingertips

1 teaspoon kosher salt

¼ teaspoon freshly ground black pepper

1 tablespoon chopped fresh rosemary

1 tablespoon chopped fresh thyme

¼ cup pimento-stuffed green olives, drained and finely minced in a food processor

2 fresh bay leaves

½ cup grated Parmesan cheese

Preheat the oven to 250°F.

In a large bowl, combine the cereals, corn snacks, cracker squares, pretzel sticks, almonds, and pumpkin seeds and stir to mix.

In a small saucepan, melt the butter with the olive oil, Worcestershire sauce, onion and garlic powders, paprika, dried orange peel, sage, salt, and pepper over medium heat. When the butter has melted and the mixture is hot, remove from the heat and stir to combine. Stir in the rosemary, thyme, and olives. Drizzle the seasoning mixture over the cereal mixture and toss gently to coat evenly. Add the bay leaves and cheese and toss again.

Divide the mixture evenly between 2 rimmed baking sheets. Bake, stirring once or twice, until crisped and golden, about 1 hour. Remove from the oven and let cool completely. The mixture may be stored in an airtight container at room temperature for up to 1 week.

# Green Bean Gratin

Sure, people love the old-fashioned version made with canned mushroom soup. But if you're looking to switch things up a bit this year, try this rich, creamy casserole made with fresh mushrooms and tangy Boursin cheese.

**SERVES 12 TO 15**

6 tablespoons butter, plus more for the baking dish

2 pounds green beans, trimmed and cut into 2-inch pieces

¾ cup minced shallots

1 red bell pepper, seeded and finely diced

8 ounces mixed mushrooms such as oyster, cremini, and shiitake, sliced

Kosher salt

2 tablespoons all-purpose flour

¼ cup dry sherry

2 cups whole milk

1 (5¼-ounce) round Boursin cheese

¼ teaspoon freshly ground black pepper

Grated zest of 1 lemon

2 tablespoons chopped fresh tarragon

¾ cup *panko* (Japanese bread crumbs)

¾ cup grated Parmesan cheese

¾ cup sliced almonds

Preheat the oven to 375°F. Butter a 9-by-13-inch baking dish.

Bring a large pot three-fourths full of salted water to a rolling boil over high heat. Prepare an ice bath. Add the beans to the boiling water and cook until tender, 3 to 5 minutes. Drain the beans, then plunge them into the ice bath to halt the cooking. When the beans are fully chilled, drain and set aside.

In a large, heavy-bottomed saucepan, melt 4 tablespoons of the butter over medium-high heat. Add the shallots and cook, stirring occasionally, until translucent, 2 to 3 minutes. Add the bell pepper and mushrooms and a pinch of salt and cook, stirring occasionally, until the vegetables have softened and the mushrooms have given up their liquid, about 5 minutes. Stir in the flour and cook, stirring, for 1 minute more. Stir in the sherry, mixing well, then add the milk while whisking constantly. Bring to a simmer, stirring occasionally. Reduce the heat to medium-low and cook, stirring, until thickened, about 1 minute, then continue to cook for 3 minutes longer.

Remove from the heat and whisk in the Boursin cheese, 1 teaspoon salt, the pepper, the lemon zest, and the tarragon. Taste and adjust the seasoning with salt and pepper if needed. Add the reserved green beans and toss to combine. Transfer the mixture to the prepared baking dish. (The recipe may be prepared up to this point, covered, and refrigerated for up to 2 days before continuing.)

**To finish the casserole:** In a small bowl, stir together the *panko*, Parmesan cheese, and almonds. In a small pan, melt the remaining 2 tablespoons butter, pour over the bread crumb mixture, and toss to combine. Sprinkle the crumb topping evenly over the green beans.

Bake until the topping is golden and the bean mixture is bubbling, about 30 minutes. Serve immediately.

# Oven-Baked Stuffing

For traditionalists, it doesn't get any more classic than this simple, satisfying stuffing made with cubes of crusty bread, plenty of celery, and the familiar flavors of sage and thyme.

**SERVES 12 TO 15**

¾ cup butter, plus more for the baking dish

1 large loaf good-quality Italian or French bread, cut into ½-inch cubes (about 12 cups)

7 large celery stalks, coarsely chopped (about 2 cups)

2 cups coarsely chopped onion

½ teaspoon dried sage, rubbed between fingertips

½ teaspoon dried thyme, rubbed between fingertips

1 teaspoon salt

¼ teaspoon freshly ground black pepper

2 cups chicken broth, plus more if needed

Preheat the oven to 300°F. Butter a 9-by-13-inch baking dish.

Divide the bread cubes between 2 rimmed baking sheets. Place the pans in the oven and bake, stirring occasionally, until the bread is completely dry but has not taken on color, about 30 minutes. Remove from the oven and set aside. Raise the oven temperature to 375°F.

Place the celery in a food processor and pulse to chop finely. Scrape the chopped celery and any accumulated juices into a bowl. Add the onion to the food processor and pulse to chop finely, stopping once to scrape down the sides of the processor if necessary. Scrape the onion and any accumulated juices into the bowl with the celery.

In a large pot, melt the butter over medium heat. Add the onion-celery mixture and its juices and cook slowly, stirring occasionally, until the vegetables are completely softened but have not taken on color, about 20 minutes. Remove from the heat.

Stir the sage, thyme, salt, and pepper into the vegetable mixture. Add the dried bread cubes and stir to combine. Add the broth and stir until the bread has absorbed all of the liquid. Taste the stuffing for seasoning and adjust with salt and pepper if needed. If the stuffing is still a bit dry, add more broth (it should be well moistened but not mushy). Transfer the stuffing to the prepared baking dish and cover tightly with aluminum foil.

Place the stuffing in the oven and bake for 30 minutes. Remove the foil and continue to bake until the top starts to brown, about 15 minutes longer. Serve right away.

# Sausage and Ricotta Stuffing
## with Swiss Chard and Fontina

This stuffing is richer and more substantial than the Oven-Baked Stuffing (page 33). If you're cooking for a big crowd with a range of ages and tastes, why not make both? For extra color, use rainbow chard.

**SERVES 12 TO 15**

Butter for the baking dish

1 large loaf good-quality Italian or French bread, cut into ½-inch cubes (about 12 cups)

1 tablespoon olive oil, plus more if needed

1 pound mild Italian sausages, casings removed

1 cup finely chopped onions

1 cup finely chopped celery

1 tablespoon finely minced garlic

2 bunches Swiss chard, trimmed and cut into 1-inch pieces

1½ teaspoons kosher salt

2 large eggs

1 cup part-skim ricotta cheese

3 cups chicken broth, plus more if needed

1 tablespoon chopped fresh thyme

½ teaspoon freshly ground black pepper

6 ounces Fontina cheese, shredded (about 1½ cups)

Nonstick cooking spray

Preheat the oven to 300°F. Butter a 9-by-13-inch baking dish.

Divide the bread cubes between 2 rimmed baking sheets. Place the pans in the oven and bake, stirring occasionally, until the bread is completely dry but has not taken on color, about 30 minutes. Remove from the oven and set aside. Raise the oven temperature to 375°F.

In a large skillet, heat the olive oil over medium-high heat. Add the sausage and cook, breaking up any clumps into small pieces with a wooden spoon, until well browned, 7 to 8 minutes. Using a slotted spoon, transfer the sausage to a large bowl and set aside.

You want 2 tablespoons fat remaining in the skillet. If you have less than that, add olive oil as needed. Return the pan to medium-high heat, add the onions and celery, and cook, stirring occasionally, until the celery and onions are soft and the onions are translucent, about 5 minutes. Add the garlic and cook 2 minutes more. Add the chard and ½ teaspoon of the salt and cook until the chard wilts and is tender, 6 to 7 minutes.

Remove the pan from the heat and transfer the contents to a colander set in the sink to drain off any excess liquid, pressing on the greens with the back of a wooden spoon. You should have about 2 cups greens. Set aside.

In a medium bowl, whisk the eggs until blended. Add the ricotta and 2 cups of the broth and whisk until smooth. Whisk in the thyme, the remaining 1 teaspoon salt, and the pepper and mix well.

Add the reserved bread cubes, cooked chard, and Fontina to the bowl with the sausage and toss to combine. Then pour the ricotta mixture over the stuffing and toss to mix thoroughly. If the stuffing seems a little dry, add more broth a little at a time until the stuffing seems moistened but not wet. Transfer the mixture to the prepared baking dish. Spray a sheet of aluminum foil with nonstick spray and cover the dish, sprayed side down.

Place the stuffing in the oven and bake for 30 minutes. Remove the foil and continue to bake until the top is browned, about 10 minutes longer. Serve right away.

# Roasted Sweet Potatoes with
## Red Pears and Balsamic Glaze

If you like mashed sweet potatoes, go directly to page 65. But if roasted root vegetables are more to your liking, give these easy, yet sophisticated sweet potatoes a try.

**SERVES 12 TO 15**

½ cup pecan halves

4 large sweet potatoes, about 3½ pounds total weight, peeled and cut into 1-inch cubes

4 slightly underripe red pears such as red Anjou or red Bartlett, halved, cored, and cut into 1-inch cubes

8 shallots, quartered

¼ cup olive oil

1½ teaspoons salt

½ teaspoon freshly ground black pepper

1 teaspoon dried thyme, rubbed between your fingertips

3 to 4 tablespoons good-quality balsamic vinegar

1 small head radicchio, cored and very thinly sliced (about 4 cups loosely packed)

¼ cup chopped fresh sage

Preheat the oven to 325°F.

Spread the pecans on a small rimmed baking sheet, place in the oven, and toast, shaking the pan occasionally, until the nuts take on color and are fragrant, 15 to 20 minutes. Remove from the oven, let cool, and then coarsely chop. Set aside for garnish. Raise the oven temperature to 450°F.

In a large bowl, combine the sweet potatoes, pears, and shallots. Drizzle with the olive oil, sprinkle with the salt, pepper, and thyme, and toss to distribute the oil and seasonings evenly.

Divide the mixture evenly between 2 rimmed baking sheets and spread in a single, even layer on each sheet. Make sure the vegetables and pears aren't too crowded so they will roast evenly. Roast until browned and tender, about 30 minutes.

Using a metal spatula, transfer the vegetables and pears to a warmed serving bowl, being careful to scrape up all the tasty browned bits on each pan bottom. Add 3 tablespoons of the vinegar, the radicchio, and the sage and toss well to combine. Taste and adjust with more vinegar, salt, and pepper if needed. Garnish with the pecans and serve immediately.

# Mashed Potatoes Three Ways

It just isn't Thanksgiving without a big bowl of buttery mashed potatoes. Here's a reliable way to get them just right, plus two simple ideas for dressing them up. All three versions can be made up to 2 days in advance and reheated at serving time.

**SERVES 12 TO 15**

5 pounds baking potatoes, peeled and cut into chunks

1 tablespoon plus 2 teaspoons kosher salt

½ cup butter

1 cup heavy cream

1 cup whole milk

Freshly ground black pepper (optional)

In a large pot, combine the potatoes with water just to cover. Add 1 tablespoon of the salt and bring to a boil over high heat. Reduce the heat slightly and cook until the potatoes are easily pierced with a fork, 12 to 15 minutes. While the potatoes are cooking, in a small saucepan, warm together the butter, cream, and milk over low heat until the butter is melted.

Set a colander in the sink and drain the potatoes. Put the drained potatoes back into the pot, return the pot to the stove top over high heat, and heat, shaking the pot occasionally, to evaporate any excess moisture, about 30 seconds. Pass the potato chunks through a food mill or a ricer placed over a large bowl, then stir in the warm butter mixture. Season with the remaining 2 teaspoons salt and with the pepper, if using, then taste and adjust the seasoning if needed.

Transfer to a warmed serving bowl and serve right away. Or, let cool to room temperature, cover, and refrigerate for up to 2 days, then reheat in a microwave, stirring once or twice, until hot.

**Whole-Grain Mustard and Thyme Variation:** After stirring in the butter mixture, stir in ¼ cup whole-grain mustard and 1 tablespoon chopped fresh thyme.

**Buttermilk and Chive Variation:** Substitute 1 cup buttermilk for the milk. After stirring in the butter mixture, stir in ¼ cup finely sliced fresh chives.

**TIP:** To make an easy post-Thanksgiving shepherd's pie, mix leftover turkey and gravy with some sautéed onions, celery, carrots, and peas. Spoon into a baking dish, cover with leftover mashed potatoes, dot the top with butter, and bake in a moderate oven until bubbly and lightly browned.

# Classic Cranberry Sauce

**MAKES ABOUT 2 CUPS**

1 (12-ounce) bag fresh cranberries (about 3 cups)

1 cup fresh orange juice, apple cider (preferably unfiltered), or pomegranate juice

¾ cup sugar

1 tablespoon grated orange zest

1 cinnamon stick

Pinch of kosher salt

In a heavy-bottomed saucepan, combine the cranberries, orange juice, sugar, orange zest, cinnamon stick, and salt and bring to a boil over medium heat. Reduce the heat to low and simmer until the sauce has thickened and all of the berries have burst, about 15 minutes.

Remove from the heat, let cool, and remove and discard the cinnamon stick. Serve immediately. Or, cover and refrigerate for up to 4 days, then bring to room temperature before serving.

If you've never made cranberry sauce, you'll be amazed at how easy it is. And that fresh flavor and "pop" of the berries beat the canned stuff hands down.

Glazing the turkey as it roasts with a mixture of apple cider, butter, and mustard gives it a richly caramelized color and makes for some of the most flavorful pan gravy you'll ever taste.

# Cider-Glazed Turkey with Perfect Pan Gravy

**SERVES 12 TO 15**

### CIDER GLAZE

3 cups apple cider (preferably unfiltered)

½ cup butter, cubed

1 tablespoon Dijon mustard

1 whole turkey, 18 to 20 pounds, thawed if frozen

Kosher salt and freshly ground black pepper

1 large apple, cut into eighths

2 shallots, halved

4 fresh rosemary sprigs

4 fresh sage sprigs

2 bay leaves

6 cups chicken broth

1 onion, chopped

2 celery stalks, chopped

2 carrots, peeled and chopped

6 cups water

½ cup all-purpose flour

1 tablespoon Dijon mustard

Preheat the oven to 325°F. Place a V rack large enough to hold the turkey in a roasting pan.

**For the cider glaze:** In a medium saucepan, bring the cider to a boil over high heat. Reduce the heat to medium and simmer until reduced by half (1½ cups), about 20 minutes. Add the butter and whisk until melted. Remove from the heat and whisk in the mustard. Set aside.

**For the turkey:** If the turkey has a metal clamp on its legs, remove it. Remove the giblets and neck from the cavity.

Discard the liver or reserve for another use and set the neck and giblets aside for making the gravy. Rinse the bird well and pat dry with paper towels. Season the inside of the turkey liberally with salt and pepper. Stuff the apple, shallots, rosemary, sage, and bay leaves into the cavity of the bird and truss the legs together. Place the turkey, breast side up, in the rack in the roasting pan. Generously brush the outside of the bird all over with some of the cider glaze and season liberally with salt and pepper.

Place the bird in the oven and roast for 1 hour. Baste with the remaining cider glaze, pouring all of it over the bird. Tent the bird with foil if it is starting to look too brown; add 2 cups of the broth to the bottom of the pan. Return the bird to the oven and continue to roast for 3 to 4 hours longer, basting every 45 minutes or so with the pan juices. The turkey is done if when a thigh joint is pierced the juices run clear, or when an instant-read thermometer inserted into the thickest part of a thigh away from bone registers 165°F.

**While the bird is cooking, make the giblet broth:** In a large saucepan, combine the reserved giblets and neck, onion, celery, carrots, water, and the remaining 4 cups broth. Bring to a boil over medium-high heat, reduce the heat to a gentle simmer, and cook, uncovered, for 1½ hours. Remove the giblet broth from the heat and strain through a fine-mesh sieve. You should have about 4 cups. Set aside for making the gravy.

When the turkey has finished cooking, transfer it to a carving board, tent it with aluminum foil, and let rest for 20 to 30 minutes before carving.

**While the bird is resting, make the gravy:** Pour the drippings from the roasting pan into a 1-quart measuring cup and wait for a few minutes for the fat to rise to the surface. Carefully spoon off the fat, discarding all but 5 tablespoons. You should have about 3 cups pan juices. Pour a little of the reserved giblet broth into the bottom of the roasting pan, scrape up any browned bits, and add to the pan drippings. Strain the pan juice–broth mixture through a fine-mesh sieve into a 2-quart measuring cup, then add enough of the giblet broth to total 6 cups liquid. Set aside.

In a saucepan, heat the reserved 5 tablespoons fat over medium heat. Add the flour and cook, stirring constantly, until the fat and flour have thickened and are starting to smell a little toasty, 1 to 2 minutes. Slowly whisk in the 6 cups pan juice–broth mixture and bring to a simmer. Reduce the heat to low and simmer for 10 minutes, whisking occasionally. Whisk in the mustard, taste for seasoning, and adjust with salt and pepper if needed. If the gravy seems too thick, add a little more of the giblet broth. You should have about 6 cups gravy. Keep warm.

Carve the turkey and serve. Pour the gravy into a warmed serving bowl and pass at the table.

# All-American Apple Pie

**SERVES 8 TO 12**

## CRUST

3 cups all-purpose flour

2 tablespoons sugar

Generous pinch of salt

¾ cup cold unsalted butter, cubed

¾ cup frozen solid vegetable shortening, cubed

7 to 9 tablespoons ice water

## FILLING

4 pounds Granny Smith apples, peeled, cored, and thinly sliced

¾ cup sugar

2 tablespoons cornstarch

1 teaspoon ground cinnamon

¼ teaspoon salt

Juice of ½ lemon

1 large egg

1 tablespoon water

2 teaspoons sugar

Whipped cream, vanilla ice cream, or sharp Cheddar cheese for serving

**For the crust:** In a food processor, combine the flour, sugar, and salt and pulse a few times to combine. Scatter the butter and shortening over the top and pulse about 10 times until the mixture resembles a coarse meal. Sprinkle with 7 tablespoons of the ice water and pulse a few more times. Press a little of the dough together with your hand. If it holds together, it is ready. If it falls apart, sprinkle in a little more ice water and pulse just to incorporate.

Gather up the dough into a ball, divide it in half, and flatten each half into a disk about 5 inches in diameter. Wrap the disks separately with plastic wrap and refrigerate for at least 1 hour or up to 3 days.

Preheat the oven to 425°F.

Remove the dough from the refrigerator. If it is very stiff, allow it to warm up for 10 minutes before rolling. On a lightly floured work surface, using a floured rolling pin, roll out 1 dough disk into a 12-inch circle about ⅛ inch thick. Fold the circle in half and carefully transfer it to a 9-inch pie pan. Unfold the circle and gently press the dough into the bottom and sides of the pan, leaving a ½-inch overhang around the rim. Place the pan in the refrigerator while you prepare the apple filling.

**For the filling:** In a large bowl, combine the apple slices, sugar, cornstarch, cinnamon, salt, and lemon juice and toss well to coat the apples evenly. Mound the mixture in the pastry-lined pan, being sure to scrape in any liquid that has accumulated in the bowl.

**To finish the pie:** Roll out the second dough disk in the same manner as the first. Fold the dough circle in half and carefully transfer it to the pie pan, centering the midline of the halved circle over the apples. Unfold the circle and, using kitchen shears, trim the overhanging edges of the top and bottom crusts to ½ inch. Press the edges of the crusts together with your fingers, and tuck them under so they are flush with the lip of the pie pan. Using the tines of a fork, press the dough around the rim of the pan to make a decorative edge. Using a 2-inch biscuit cutter or sharp paring knife, cut a round vent in the center of the top crust of the pie. In a small bowl, whisk together the egg and water to make a wash. Brush the entire top crust lightly with the egg wash, then sprinkle with the sugar.

Bake the pie for 30 minutes. Reduce the oven temperature to 375°F and continue to bake until the crust is golden brown and you can see the juices bubbling through the vent, about 30 minutes longer. Let the pie cool on a rack for 2 hours before serving.

Cut the pie into wedges and accompany each wedge with a dollop of whipped cream, a scoop of vanilla ice cream, or a slice of Cheddar.

This traditional double-crust pie is light on the spices, so the flavor of the apples really shines through. It bakes up proud and tall—the perfect centerpiece for a dessert buffet.

# EMERIL LAGASSE
# PARADE PARTY

If you've got friends and family in town for the Thanksgiving week-end or a houseful of holiday guests, Emeril's easy, casual, mostly made-ahead menu is the perfect way to start the season: a brunch of comforting hot and cold favorites to enjoy while watching the parade on TV.

"It only takes three ingredients to make this sophisticated, totally refreshing brunch cocktail that's a great choice for adding a little sparkle to any holiday gathering. And it's so quick, you can make each drink to order as your guests arrive without missing a beat."

## Sparkling Prosecco Cocktail

**SERVES 8**

About 1 cup mango, orange, grapefruit, or raspberry sorbet

½ cup liqueur such as Chambord, Grand Marnier, or framboise

1 (750-ml) bottle Prosecco or other sparkling wine

Using a very small ice-cream scoop or a tablespoon, place 1 scoop of sorbet into the bottom of each of 8 Champagne flutes. Add 1 tablespoon of the liqueur to each glass, then fill the glasses with the Prosecco, dividing it evenly. Serve right away.

"Here's a foolproof way to make individual servings of eggs when you've got a crowd to feed. People always love getting their own ramekin of custardy, creamy goodness."

"Sure you can buy chicken-apple sausages. But once you try my easy version, you may never settle for store-bought again. They're moist and flavorful, with just the right spicy jalapeño kick."

# **Coddled Eggs** with Fresh Herbs

**SERVES 6**

2 tablespoons unsalted butter, at room temperature

6 large eggs

½ cup plus 1 tablespoon heavy cream

2 tablespoons grated Parmesan cheese

2 tablespoons chopped fresh chives

1½ tablespoons chopped fresh flat-leaf parsley

1 teaspoon chopped fresh lemon thyme or thyme

Salt and freshly ground black pepper

Preheat the oven to 350°F. Butter six ¾- or 1-cup ramekins with the butter.

**To assemble the ramekins:** Carefully crack 1 egg into each ramekin. Spoon 1½ tablespoons of the heavy cream over each egg, then sprinkle 1 teaspoon of the Parmesan cheese over each egg. In a small bowl, mix together the chives, parsley, and thyme. Divide the herbs evenly among the ramekins, sprinkling them over the eggs. Season each egg lightly with salt and pepper.

**To bake and serve the ramekins:** Transfer the ramekins to a 9-by-13-inch baking pan with 2-inch sides, spacing them so their sides do not touch one another. Open the oven door and pull out the center oven rack most of the way, but not so far that it will tip when the pan is set on it. Set the pan holding the ramekins on the rack and pour hot water into the pan to reach halfway up the sides of the ramekins. Cover the pan with aluminum foil. Slowly slide the rack into the oven, and close the oven door. Bake the eggs until the whites are gently set but the yolks are still soft, 17 to 20 minutes.

Carefully remove the baking pan from the oven and uncover. Remove the ramekins from the pan and serve right away.

# **Organic-Chicken Breakfast Sausage Patties**

**SERVES 6**

4 tablespoons vegetable oil

½ cup chopped onions

½ cup chopped red bell peppers

2 tablespoons chopped, seeded jalapeño chile

2 tablespoons chopped celery

1 teaspoon salt

1 tablespoon minced garlic

¼ cup chopped walnuts (optional)

1 pound ground lean organic chicken (85 percent lean)

2 tablespoons chopped fresh cilantro or other soft herb of choice

¼ cup finely chopped, peeled apple

In a 12-inch nonstick skillet, heat 2 tablespoons of the vegetable oil over medium heat. Add the onions, bell peppers, chile, celery, and salt and cook, stirring often, until soft, 3 to 4 minutes. Add the garlic and the walnuts, if using, and cook for 1 minute longer. Remove the pan from the heat, transfer the onion mixture to a medium bowl, and set aside to cool. Wipe the skillet clean and set it aside until needed.

Add the chicken, cilantro, and apple to the cooled onion mixture. With gloved hands or a spoon, gently combine the ingredients until they are uniformly blended. Then divide the mixture into 6 equal portions (about 3½ ounces each) and form each portion into a patty about 4 inches in diameter.

Set the skillet over medium heat and add 1 tablespoon of the vegetable oil. When the oil is hot, add 3 of the patties and cook, turning once, until golden brown and cooked through, 4 to 5 minutes on each side. Transfer to a warmed plate and tent with aluminum foil to keep warm. Repeat with the remaining 3 patties and 1 tablespoon oil. Serve right away.

# Homemade Granola with Honey-Vanilla Greek Yogurt and Mixed-Berry Salad

### HOMEMADE GRANOLA

Nonstick cooking spray

1½ cups old-fashioned rolled oats

¼ cup chopped almonds

¼ cup chopped walnuts

2 tablespoons flaxseeds

2 tablespoons sunflower seeds

2 tablespoons pumpkin seeds

1 tablespoon firmly packed dark brown sugar

¼ teaspoon ground cinnamon

¼ teaspoon salt

¼ cup honey

2 tablespoons agave nectar

1 tablespoon grapeseed oil

½ teaspoon pure vanilla extract

¼ cup dried cranberries

¼ cup raisins

### HONEY-VANILLA GREEK YOGURT

2¼ cups nonfat or low-fat plain Greek yogurt

3 tablespoons honey

2½ teaspoons pure vanilla extract

### MIXED-BERRY SALAD

1 pound strawberries (about 4 cups)

1 cup raspberries

1 cup blackberries

1 tablespoon plus 1 teaspoon agave nectar

1 tablespoon finely chopped fresh mint

**For the granola:** Preheat the oven to 325°F. Spray a rimmed baking sheet with nonstick spray.

In a medium bowl, combine the oats, almonds, walnuts, flaxseeds, sunflower seeds, pumpkin seeds, brown sugar, cinnamon, and salt and stir to mix well. In a small bowl, stir together the honey, agave nectar, grapeseed oil, and vanilla and mix well. Add the honey mixture to the oat mixture and stir until well mixed.

Turn the mixture out onto the prepared baking sheet and spread into an even layer with a rubber spatula. Bake, stirring once after 10 to 12 minutes, until the mixture is golden brown, about 22 minutes.

Remove from the oven and break up any large pieces. While the granola is still warm, stir in the cranberries and raisins. Let the granola cool completely, then transfer to an airtight container until serving. It will keep at room temperature for up to 2 weeks.

**For the yogurt:** In a medium bowl, combine the yogurt, honey, and vanilla and stir together with a rubber spatula until combined. Cover and refrigerate until serving.

**For the berry salad:** Gently wash the strawberries, raspberries, and blackberries and lay them on a baking sheet lined with paper towels to dry.

Hull the strawberries and cut lengthwise into ¼-inch-thick slices. Place them in a large bowl and add the raspberries and blackberries. Drizzle the agave nectar over the berries and add the mint. Using a rubber spatula, toss gently but thoroughly to combine. Set the bowl aside at room temperature for about 30 minutes before serving to allow the flavors to come together.

**To serve:** Spoon an equal amount of the yogurt into each of 6 to 8 small bowls or parfait glasses. Top with some of the mixed berries, then garnish with the granola to taste.

"Granola parfaits look and taste great, and they go together quickly at the last minute. Packed in jars and tied with a ribbon, my easy granola makes a nice gift all through the holidays."

# Breakfast Casserole with
# Broccoli, Ham, and Cheese

"This casserole is packed with broccoli and lighter on eggs than the usual savory bread pudding, so it won't fill you up before the big meal later in the day."

**SERVES 6 TO 8**

Nonstick cooking spray

1¼ teaspoons salt, plus more to season

6 cups broccoli florets (from about 2 pounds broccoli heads)

1 tablespoon olive oil

1½ cups finely chopped onions

1¼ cups (about 8 ounces) finely chopped ham

3 cups shredded Cheddar cheese

8 cups cubed crusty bread such as French or Italian (1-inch cubes)

8 large eggs, lightly beaten

3 cups half-and-half

2 tablespoons minced fresh chives or scallions (white and tender green parts)

1¼ teaspoons sweet paprika

¼ teaspoon cayenne pepper

¾ cup grated Parmesan cheese

**To assemble the casserole:** Spray a 9-by-13-inch baking dish with nonstick spray. Fill a large pot three-fourths full of water and bring to a boil over high heat. Meanwhile, prepare an ice bath. Season the water with salt, add the broccoli florets, and blanch until bright green and barely tender, about 1 minute. Using a skimmer, transfer the broccoli to the ice bath to halt the cooking. When the broccoli is fully chilled, drain well, pat dry with paper towels, and set aside.

In a small sauté pan, heat the olive oil over medium-high heat. Add the onions and a couple of pinches of salt and cook, stirring occasionally, until the onions are soft, about 4 minutes. Remove from the heat and set aside to cool.

In a large bowl, combine the broccoli, cooled onions, ham, Cheddar cheese, and bread cubes. Toss gently to combine, then transfer to the prepared baking dish, spreading the mixture in an even layer.

Using the same bowl, whisk together the eggs, half-and-half, chives, 1¼ teaspoons salt, paprika, and cayenne pepper until thoroughly mixed. Pour over the broccoli mixture. Cover with plastic wrap and store in the refrigerator for at least 4 hours or up to overnight. About 30 minutes before baking, remove the casserole from the refrigerator and allow to come to room temperature.

**To bake the casserole:** Preheat the oven to 375°F. Remove the plastic wrap from the baking dish and cover the dish with aluminum foil. Place in the oven and bake for 45 minutes. Remove the foil and sprinkle the Parmesan cheese evenly over the top. Return the casserole, uncovered, to the oven and continue baking until the top is golden brown and puffed and the casserole is cooked through when tested with a knife, about 15 minutes longer.

Transfer the casserole to a rack and let rest for 10 to 15 minutes before serving. Cut into squares to serve.

## TOM DOUGLAS

# LEFT COAST THANKSGIVING

Tom closes all of his restaurants on Thanksgiving and heads home for a friends-and-family dinner that celebrates the bounty of the Pacific Northwest. For him, the highlight of the meal is having guests read "food and gratitude" excerpts from books in his extensive kitchen library. Here's a menu inspired by some of his favorite local ingredients.

# Togarashi Prawns with Tangerine-Ginger Glaze

"*Togarashi* is kind of like the salt and pepper of Japan. You can make your own, or look for it in little shaker bottles in Asian grocery stores or online."

**SERVES 8**

**TOGARASHI**

2 sheets nori

2 tablespoons sesame seeds, toasted

2 tablespoons grated orange zest, spread on a paper towel to dry

2 tablespoons red pepper flakes

**TANGERINE-GINGER GLAZE**

2 cups fresh tangerine juice

1 cup mirin

½ cup soy sauce

¼ cup firmly packed light brown sugar

2 tablespoons granulated sugar

4 teaspoons grated, peeled fresh ginger

1 teaspoon chopped garlic

1 teaspoon grated tangerine zest

2 teaspoons cornstarch

2 teaspoons water

2 pounds large prawns, peeled and deveined, tail segments attached

Kosher salt and freshly ground pepper

Preheat a gas grill to medium-high, or light a fire in a charcoal grill and let it burn just until the coals are covered with gray ash and very hot.

For the *togarashi:* Preheat the oven to 350°F. Lay the nori on an ungreased baking sheet. Place in the oven until toasted, about 20 minutes. Remove from the oven, let the nori cool, then rip it into pieces that will fit in your spice grinder. Working in batches if necessary, finely grind the nori, sesame seeds, orange zest, and red pepper flakes. Transfer to a small bowl and mix well.

For the glaze: In a small saucepan, combine the tangerine juice, mirin, soy sauce, both sugars, ginger, garlic, and tangerine zest and place over medium heat. Bring to a simmer, stirring until the sugar dissolves, and simmer until reduced by half, 12 to 15 minutes.

In a small bowl, stir together the cornstarch and water. Add the mixture to the simmering reduced glaze and simmer for 1 minute. The glaze should be as thick as maple syrup. Remove from the heat and let cool for a few minutes. Pour one-fourth of the glaze into a small bowl and reserve.

To grill: Brush the prawns on both sides with the remaining glaze, and sprinkle them with the *togarashi*, salt, and pepper. Working in batches, place on the grill grate and grill, turning often, until firm and pink, 3 to 4 minutes.

Transfer the prawns to a warmed platter and spoon the reserved glaze evenly over the top.

# Washington Apple Salad

"In the fall and winter, apples are a great way to add freshness and crunch to a salad. Cougar Gold is a crumbly aged Cheddar made by the Washington State University Creamery. They've been packing it in cans since World War II."

**SERVES 8**

**HAZELNUT CIDER VINAIGRETTE**

1 tablespoon minced shallot

1 tablespoon Dijon mustard

2 teaspoons honey

2 teaspoons chopped fresh thyme

¼ cup cider vinegar

¾ cup olive oil

Kosher salt and freshly ground pepper

4 Washington apples such as Honeycrisp, halved, cored, and julienned

4 cups loosely packed frisée leaves

4 heads Belgian endive, cored and chopped

½ fennel bulb, cored and thinly sliced crosswise

8 ounces aged sharp Cheddar cheese, preferably Cougar Gold, crumbled

In a small bowl, whisk together the shallot, mustard, honey, thyme, and vinegar. Gradually whisk in the olive oil to form an emulsion. Season with salt and pepper.

In a large bowl, combine the apples, frisée, endive, and fennel. Drizzle with about two-thirds of the vinaigrette and toss to coat all of the ingredients lightly, adding more of the vinaigrette as needed. You may not need all of the vinaigrette. Season with salt and pepper.

Divide the salad among chilled individual plates, and sprinkle each serving with an equal amount of the cheese. Serve right away.

# Best-of-the-Northwest Stuffing with Dried Cherries, Hazelnuts, and Oyster Mushrooms

**SERVES 8**

1 cup hazelnuts

½ cup unsalted butter, plus more for buttering the pan

1 loaf coarse country bread, 1 to 1¼ pounds

3 tablespoons olive oil

Kosher salt and freshly ground black pepper

½ cup finely chopped shallots

1 pound oyster mushrooms, stems trimmed and coarsely chopped

⅔ cup dried cherries or dried cranberries, soaked in hot water for 15 minutes and drained

⅓ cup finely chopped fresh flat-leaf parsley

¼ cup finely sliced fresh chives

2 tablespoons finely chopped fresh thyme

2 teaspoons grated orange zest

2 cups homemade turkey or chicken stock or purchased low-sodium broth, heated

Preheat the oven to 350°F.

Spread the hazelnuts on a rimmed baking sheet and place in the oven until they take on color and are fragrant, 10 to 15 minutes. Remove from the oven and pour the nuts onto the center of a clean kitchen towel. Wrap the warm nuts in the towel and rub the nuts between your palms to remove as much of the thin, papery skins as possible. Pour the nuts onto a cutting board and chop them. Measure ⅔ cup and set aside. Reserve any remaining toasted nuts for another use.

Raise the oven temperature to 375°F. Butter a 9-by-13-inch baking dish or similar-sized shallow baking dish or pan.

Using a serrated knife, slice both ends off of the bread loaf, then slice off the heaviest, thickest parts of the crust (remove the bottom crust plus any very thick parts or ridges from the top crust, but don't worry about removing every bit of the crust). Cut the bread into 1- to 1½-inch chunks. You should have about 10 cups. Put the bread in a large bowl, drizzle with the olive oil, and toss to coat the bread chunks evenly. Season with salt and pepper. Spread the bread on a rimmed baking sheet, place in the oven, and toast, stirring occasionally, until golden, about 20 minutes. Remove from the oven and set aside. Reduce the oven temperature to 350°F.

In a large skillet, melt the butter over medium-high heat. Add the shallots and cook, stirring occasionally, until softened, 1 to 2 minutes. Add the mushrooms and cook, stirring occasionally, until softened and lightly browned, 8 to 10 minutes. Season with salt and pepper and remove from the heat.

In a large bowl, combine the toasted bread, mushroom-shallot mixture (use a rubber spatula to scrape all of the butter and mushroom juices from the skillet), hazelnuts, cherries, parsley, chives, thyme, and orange zest. Gradually add the stock, stirring so the bread absorbs most of the liquid. Season with salt and pepper. Spread the stuffing in the prepared baking dish and cover with aluminum foil.

Bake for 25 minutes. Remove the foil and continue to bake until the top is crusty and golden, about 35 minutes longer. Remove from the oven and serve right away

"I always cook the stuffing separately. The bird roasts more evenly, and you get a nice crunchy crust on the stuffing. Use a sturdy, rustic loaf here, and don't be shy about letting the top get really brown and crisp. You've got plenty of gravy to soften it up."

"Seattle is famous for its coffee. And that inspired me to stuff the turkey cavity with whole roasted coffee beans. Turns out they add a nice toasty-smoky aroma that seasons the bird from within. I leave them in even after the turkey's done. If a few slip out at the table while I'm carving, it's a good conversation starter."

# Coffee-Bean Turkey with Sweet Onion Gravy

**SERVES 12**

1 fresh whole turkey, 15 pounds

6 tablespoons butter, at room temperature, plus 6 tablespoons melted

Kosher salt and freshly ground black pepper

12 sage leaves

½ cup dark-roast coffee beans

1 tablespoon rendered bacon fat, melted

1 onion, cut in half lengthwise and julienned

5 cloves garlic, peeled but left whole

7 to 8 cups chicken or turkey broth, heated

½ cup instant (quick-dissolving) flour such as Wondra

Preheat the oven to 350°F.

If the turkey has a metal clamp on its legs, remove it. Remove the giblets and neck from the cavity, if included, and reserve for another use or discard. Remove the cavity fat, then rinse the turkey well and pat dry with paper towels.

In a small bowl, mash the 6 tablespoons room-temperature butter until smooth and season with salt and pepper. Using your fingers, and starting from the cavity end of the turkey, separate the skin from the breast meat, being careful not to tear the skin. Gently rub the softened butter evenly over the breast meat, then insert 6 of the sage leaves under the skin, placing 3 leaves on each breast half. Pat the skin back into place, and then brush the whole exterior of the bird with some of the melted butter. Season the turkey all over, including the cavity, with salt and pepper. Sprinkle the coffee beans inside the cavity.

**To roast the turkey:** Brush the bottom of a roasting pan just large enough to accommodate the turkey with the bacon fat, then make a bed of the onion slices in the center of the pan. Place the turkey, breast side up, on top of the onion.

Place the turkey in the oven and roast for 1 hour. Baste the turkey with some of the melted butter and add the garlic, the remaining 6 sage leaves, and 5 cups of the broth to the pan. Continue to roast the turkey, basting with butter at regular intervals a few more times, for another 1½ to 2 hours. If the turkey is browning too much, tent with aluminum foil. The turkey is done if when a thigh joint is pierced the juices run clear, or when an instant-read thermometer inserted into the thickest part of a thigh away from bone registers 155° to 165°F.

Remove the turkey from oven, transfer to a platter, and tent with aluminum foil. Let rest for about 20 minutes.

**To make the gravy:** Before beginning, remove any stray coffee beans that may have escaped from the turkey cavity into the roasting pan. Set the roasting pan with the onion slices and juices on the stove top over medium-high heat. You may need to straddle the pan over two burners. Using a wooden spoon, stir up any browned bits stuck to the pan bottom and continue stirring for a few minutes. Sprinkle the flour evenly over the onion and juices and stir until well combined, 1 to 2 minutes. Add 2 cups of the broth and any juices that have collected around the turkey on the platter, then simmer gently, whisking occasionally, until thickened, 8 to 10 minutes. If the gravy seems too thick, add more broth. Season with salt and pepper.

Pour the gravy into a warmed gravy boat and keep warm. Carve the turkey and serve immediately. Pass the gravy at the table.

**TOM'S TIP:** If you are stuffing your turkey, be careful not to overstuff it. You want plenty of space for hot air to circulate inside the cavity so the meat cooks evenly.

# Theo's Chocolate Mousse

"Theo Chocolate in Seattle is the only organic, fair-trade, beans-to-bar chocolate made in the United States. It's exceptionally good, too, and I'm not just saying that because I'm a part owner! If you can't find it for this recipe, substitute a 70 percent cacao dark chocolate you know and love."

**SERVES 6 TO 8**

### CANDIED ZEST

**4 thick-skinned oranges such as navels**

**½ cup sugar**

**½ cup water**

### CHOCOLATE MOUSSE

**4 ounces Theo bittersweet chocolate, chopped**

**2 ounces unsweetened chocolate, chopped**

**¼ cup orange liqueur such as Grand Marnier**

**3 tablespoons water**

**4 large eggs, separated**

**2 tablespoons sugar**

**1 cup heavy cream**

### ORANGE CREAM

**¾ cup heavy cream**

**1 tablespoon orange liqueur such as Grand Marnier**

**For the candied zest:** Using a 5-hole citrus zester, remove the zest from the oranges in long, narrow strips. If you don't have a zester, remove the zest in long strips with a vegetable peeler, scrape off any white pith from the underside of each strip, and then julienne each strip finely with a sharp knife. Bring a small saucepan three-fourths full of water to a boil, add the zest strips, and boil for 1 minute. Drain the zest and set aside.

Add the sugar and water to the same saucepan, place over medium-high heat, and heat, stirring occasionally, until the sugar dissolves. Add the blanched zest to the syrup, reduce the heat to a simmer, and cook until the zest is tender, about 5 minutes. Remove the pan from the heat and let the zest cool to room temperature in the syrup. Then drain the zest, reserving the candied zest and 1 tablespoon of the syrup. Set them aside separately. (The zest can be stored in an airtight container at room temperature and the syrup in an airtight container in the refrigerator. They will keep for up to 5 days.)

**For the mousse:** In a heatproof bowl, combine both chocolates, the liqueur, and the water. Place over (not touching) barely simmering water in a saucepan and heat, stirring occasionally, until the chocolate melts and the mixture is smooth. Remove the bowl from the heat and let the chocolate mixture cool slightly.

In a large bowl, whisk together the egg yolks until well combined. Using a rubber spatula, mix a small amount of the warm chocolate mixture into the yolks to temper them and prevent them from scrambling. Then add the remaining warm chocolate mixture to the egg yolks and mix with the spatula until smooth.

In a stand mixer fitted with the whisk attachment, or in a medium bowl with a handheld mixer, combine the egg whites and sugar and whip on high speed until soft peaks form. Using a hand whisk, whisk about one-fourth of the whites into the chocolate mixture to lighten it. Then, using a rubber spatula, gently but thoroughly fold about one-third of the remaining whites into the chocolate mixture. Repeat with the remaining whites in two batches.

Rinse and dry the bowl and the whisk attachment or beaters used for beating the whites. Pour the cream into the bowl and whip on high speed until soft peaks form. Using the rubber spatula, fold the whipped cream, about one-third at a time, into the chocolate–egg white mixture, folding until the mixture is smooth and no white streaks are visible. Spoon the mousse into a glass serving bowl or individual serving dishes. Cover with plastic wrap and chill for at least 3 hours or up to overnight.

**For the orange cream:** In the stand mixer fitted with the whisk attachment, or in a medium bowl with the hand-held mixer, combine the cream, liqueur, and the reserved 1 tablespoon syrup and whip on high speed until soft peaks form.

**To serve:** spoon the orange cream into a pastry bag fitted with a ½-inch star tip and pipe it decoratively over the mousse. Alternatively, attractively spoon the orange cream directly over the mousse. Arrange the candied zest over the orange cream. Serve immediately.

## MARC FORGIONE

# NEW CLASSIC
# THANKSGIVING

Growing up in a restaurant family that had a major hand in defining American cuisine (his dad is the renowned chef Larry Forgione), Marc gets the importance of respecting traditions. But he's also not afraid of bringing new life to them. His Thanksgiving menu features everyone's favorite holiday flavors with all kinds of fresh twists and tasty turns.

# Honeycrisp Apple Spiced Rum

"At our restaurant, we like the cocktails to be seasonal, just like the food. So in the fall, we make our own apple cider and use it in all kinds of drinks. Sweet-tart Honeycrisps are our go-to apple. Fujis are the only substitution I'd recommend."

**SERVES 6**

**SIMPLE SYRUP**

½ cup sugar

½ cup water

1½ cups unfiltered apple cider
(preferably from Honeycrisp apples)

1 Honeycrisp apple

1½ cups spiced rum

6 tablespoons fresh lemon juice

Ice cubes

6 rosemary sprigs

**For the simple syrup:** In a heavy-bottomed saucepan, combine the sugar and water over medium heat and bring to a boil, stirring occasionally. Continue to boil, stirring occasionally, until the sugar is dissolved, about 2 minutes. Remove from the heat and let cool to room temperature. You should have about ¾ cup syrup. Measure 6 tablespoons to use for the recipe; reserve the remainder in an airtight container in the refrigerator for a second batch of this cocktail or to sweeten other drinks. It will keep for up to several months in the refrigerator.

Pour the apple cider into a measuring pitcher or other container with a spout. Peel the apple. Using a melon baller, scoop out 6 apple balls, being careful to avoid the core. Add the apple balls to the cider and reserve.

In a small pitcher, stir together the rum, the 6 tablespoons simple syrup, and the lemon juice. Fill 6 cocktail glasses with ice. Remove the apple balls from the cider and skewer each one onto the woody end of a rosemary sprig. Add 1 sprig to each glass. Pour the apple cider into the rum mixture and stir well. Then pour the rum-cider mixture over the ice in the glasses, dividing it evenly. Serve right away.

"Instead of a whole turkey, I like to serve this leg-and-thigh roulade. The meat is more moist, and everybody gets to enjoy the dark meat, not just those two lucky people who snag the drumsticks. The gravy and roulade are both made ahead of time, which is a big help on the day."

# Turkey Leg Roulade

**SERVES 6**

### ROULADE

½ cup chopped fresh flat-leaf parsley

¼ cup chopped fresh rosemary

1 tablespoon chopped fresh thyme leaves

2 tablespoons minced shallots

1 clove garlic, minced

1 tablespoon pink peppercorns, crushed

½ cup extra virgin olive oil

2 leg-thigh portions from 1 (12- to 14-pound) free-range turkey, boned and butterflied with bones reserved

Kosher salt and freshly ground black pepper

### GRAVY

Bones from leg-thigh turkey portions, plus 1 or more turkey necks, wings, or other turkey bones

2 tablespoons canola oil

1 onion, coarsely chopped

1 carrot, peeled and coarsely chopped

1 celery stalk, coarsely chopped

1 head garlic, halved crosswise

½ cup all-purpose flour

2 cups dry white wine

5 fresh thyme sprigs

5 fresh rosemary sprigs

1 bay leaf

4 quarts organic turkey or chicken broth

Salt and freshly ground black pepper

Preheat the oven to 375°F. Place a rack on a rimmed baking sheet.

**To make the roulade, the day before serving:** In a small bowl, stir together the parsley, rosemary, thyme, shallots, garlic, peppercorns, and olive oil. Set aside.

Arrange two 18-inch squares of aluminum foil on a work surface, overlapping them slightly. Open the butterflied leg-thigh portions flat and lay them, skin side down and long sides overlapping slightly, on the foil. Season the meat generously with salt and pepper and then brush with the herb–olive oil mixture.

Working from the long edge closest to you, roll up the turkey to form a log about 4 inches in diameter and 10 inches long. Wrap the foil around the turkey and twist the ends of the foil to secure into a tight bundle. Place the bundle on the rack on the baking sheet.

Roast until an instant-read thermometer inserted (directly through the foil) into the middle of the roulade registers 145°F, about 1 hour. Remove the roulade from the oven and let cool in the foil for 40 minutes, then refrigerate overnight.

**To make the gravy, the day before serving:** Preheat the oven to 425°F. Spread the turkey bones in a roasting pan, drizzle with the canola oil, and toss to coat with the oil. Roast until browned, 30 to 45 minutes.

Transfer the roasted bones to a large stockpot, and set the roasting pan over medium heat on the stove top. Add the onion, carrot, celery, and garlic to the roasting pan and cook, stirring, until the vegetables begin to soften, 4 to 5 minutes. Sprinkle the flour over the vegetables and stir for 2 to 3 minutes. Pour in the wine and bring to a boil, stirring to dislodge any browned bits on the pan bottom. The mixture will be quite thick at this point. Transfer the vegetables and liquid to the stockpot. Add the thyme, rosemary, bay leaf, and broth to the stockpot, place over high heat, and bring to a boil. Reduce the heat to low and simmer until reduced by about half, 3 to 4 hours.

Strain the mixture through a fine-mesh sieve into a large saucepan, and discard the bones and vegetables. Place the saucepan over medium heat, bring to a simmer, and simmer until thickened enough to coat the back of a spoon, about 1 hour longer. Season to taste with salt and pepper and let cool to room temperature. You should have about 6 cups. Cover and refrigerate overnight. (The gravy may be made up to 2 days ahead of time and stored in the refrigerator.)

**To finish, 2 hours before serving:** Remove the roulade from the refrigerator and remove from the foil. Season the roulade generously with salt and pepper and let come to room temperature. Preheat the oven to 425°F. Place a rack on a rimmed baking sheet.

Place the roulade on the rack on the baking sheet and roast until an instant-read thermometer inserted into the middle of the roulade registers 140°F, about 25 minutes.

Just before the roulade is ready, lift off and discard any fat that has congealed on the surface of the gravy. Pour into a saucepan and bring to a simmer over medium heat.

To serve, cut the roulade into ¼-inch-thick slices and arrange the slices on a warmed platter. Drizzle with a little of the hot gravy and serve immediately. Pass additional gravy at the table.

**MARC'S TIPS:** You can ask your butcher to bone and butterfly the turkey leg-thigh portions, in which case you'll need about 2½ pounds (boned weight). Make sure to ask for the bones, plus a few necks or other bones, for making the gravy. The recipe makes a lot of gravy, which is perfect for leftovers. Mix some with olive oil and balsamic vinegar to make a fantastic dressing for turkey or chicken salad.

# Sunchoked Spinach with
## Farm Fresh Eggs and Bacon

"When I did the finale of *The Next Iron Chef*, the theme was Thanksgiving. I came up with a whole 1621 harvest menu based on ingredients from the first Thanksgiving. Turns out sunchokes were on the scene at Plymouth, so I used them to make this extra-luxurious creamed spinach."

**SERVES 6**

1 pound sunchokes, unpeeled, sliced crosswise ¼ inch thick

2 cups heavy cream

½ teaspoon salt, plus more to season

1 bay leaf

Unsalted butter for the baking dish

3 slices bacon, cut crosswise into ¼-inch-wide strips

2 tablespoons thinly sliced garlic

2 pounds spinach

1 cup grated Parmesan cheese, plus 1 tablespoon for garnish

1 tablespoon ground nutmeg

Salt and freshly ground black pepper

6 large farm fresh eggs (preferably organic)

¼ cup white wine vinegar

1 tablespoon *fleur de sel*

In a saucepan, combine the sunchokes, cream, ½ teaspoon salt, and bay leaf. If the sunchokes aren't submerged, add water as needed to cover. Place over medium heat, bring to a simmer, and cook until the sunchokes are completely tender and falling apart, 15 to 20 minutes.

Drain the sunchokes into a fine-mesh sieve placed over a bowl, reserving ½ cup of the cooking liquid and discarding the remaining cooking liquid and bay leaf. Transfer the sunchokes to a food processor and pulse until smooth, adding a little of the reserved cooking liquid if needed to achieve a good consistency. Reserve in the processor.

For the sunchoke-spinach base: Butter a 9-by-13-inch baking dish. In a large skillet, cook the bacon over medium heat, stirring occasionally, until browned and crisp, 5 to 6 minutes. Meanwhile, line a plate with paper towels. When the bacon is ready, using a slotted spoon, transfer half of the bacon pieces to the towel-lined plate and reserve. Add the garlic slices to the bacon remaining in the skillet and cook, stirring, until the garlic is golden, about 1 minute. Add the spinach, a few handfuls at a time,

tossing it and letting it wilt until you have room to add more. Once all of the spinach is wilted, add the contents of the skillet to the sunchoke purée in the food processor along with the 1 cup Parmesan and the nutmeg. Pulse until combined and smooth. Season to taste with salt and pepper.

Transfer the mixture to the prepared baking dish and cover to keep warm. (The recipe may be prepared up to this point 24 hours in advance, cooled, covered with aluminum foil, and stored in the refrigerator. Before serving, reheat the foil-covered dish in a preheated 375°F oven until heated through, about 30 minutes.)

To poach the eggs: Pour water to a depth of 3 inches into a wide sauce-pan or a deep sauté pan and bring to a boil over high heat. Add the vinegar and reduce the heat to a simmer. Crack each egg into its own small bowl or cup. Using a whisk, stir the water clockwise until it is spinning on its own. Then, working quickly, slip the eggs into the spinning water one at a time and cook to desired doneness, 1 to 3 minutes. Using a slotted spoon, remove the eggs from the water one at a time, blot the back of the spoon on a clean kitchen towel to absorb any excess moisture, and place on the warm spinach mixture, spacing them evenly.

Season the eggs with the *fleur de sel* and pepper, then sprinkle the dish with the reserved bacon and the remaining 1 tablespoon Parmesan. Serve right away.

# Cheddar-Chive Biscuits

"I like biscuits instead of bread at Thanksgiving. They're totally right with gravy. This recipe can be thrown together in less than 10 minutes. You can bake the biscuits in the morning and give them a quick reheat right before the meal."

**MAKES 24 BISCUITS**

3 cups all-purpose flour

1 tablespoon plus 1½ teaspoons baking powder

1 tablespoon sugar

2¼ teaspoons salt

2½ cups heavy cream

½ cup shredded sharp Cheddar cheese such as Cabot

1 cup minced fresh chives

3 tablespoons unsalted butter, melted

3 tablespoons *fleur de sel*

Preheat the oven to 350°F.

Line 2 rimmed baking sheets with parchment paper.

In a bowl, sift together the flour, baking powder, sugar, and salt. Add the cream, cheese, and chives and stir with a wooden spoon until a rough dough forms. Transfer to a lightly floured work surface and knead 5 or 6 times until the dough comes together.

Pat the dough out into a square about ½ inch thick. Using a sharp knife, trim the edges so they are even. Then, using the knife, cut 5 evenly spaced lines from one edge to the opposite edge. Now, starting on an uncut edge, cut 3 evenly spaced lines to the opposite edge. You should have 24 rectangles. Transfer the biscuits to the prepared sheet pans, spacing them at least 1 inch apart. Brush each biscuit with some of the melted butter and top with a few sprinkles of the *fleur de sel*.

Bake the biscuits, rotating the pans 180 degrees about halfway through baking, until cooked through and golden brown, 25 to 35 minutes. Remove from the oven and let cool briefly before serving. Serve warm.

"This has been a fixture on our Thanksgiving table all my life. My dad came up with it at An American Place, and everyone who tastes it swears they'll never make sweet potatoes any other way. The hazelnut brown butter is my extra spin."

# Maple Whipped Sweet Potatoes

**SERVES 6**

4 sweet potatoes, about 2½ pounds total weight, unpeeled

2 tablespoons sour cream

1 tablespoon unsalted butter, at room temperature

2 tablespoons pure maple syrup

Salt and freshly ground black pepper

HAZELNUT BROWN BUTTER

4 tablespoons unsalted butter

¼ cup chopped hazelnuts

1 small shallot, minced

2 tablespoons finely chopped fresh flat-leaf parsley

Salt and freshly ground black pepper

**For the sweet potatoes:** Preheat the oven to 375°F. Using a fork, pierce the skin of each sweet potato in a few places. Place the potatoes on a rimmed baking sheet and bake until soft, 45 to 50 minutes. Remove from the oven and let cool until they can be handled.

Cut each sweet potato in half lengthwise, scoop the potato pulp into a food processor, and discard the skin. Add the sour cream, butter, and maple syrup and pulse the mixture until smooth. Season with salt and pepper. Transfer to a baking dish and cover to keep warm until ready to serve. (The sweet potatoes may be prepared up to this point 24 hours in advance, covered, and refrigerated. To reheat, preheat the oven to 375°F, cover the baking dish with aluminum foil, and place in the oven until heated through, about 30 minutes.)

**For the brown butter:** In a heavy-bottomed saucepan, melt the butter over medium heat and cook until pale gold, 2 to 3 minutes (be careful the butter does not burn). Add the hazelnuts and stir until golden and fragrant, 1 to 2 minutes longer. Add the shallot and parsley and cook just until softened, about 1 minute. Season with salt and pepper. (The brown butter may be prepared up to 24 hours in advance, covered, and refrigerated. Before serving, reheat in a small, heavy-bottomed saucepan over medium heat.)

Drizzle the brown butter over the hot sweet potatoes and serve immediately.

# Honeycrisp Apple and Dried Fruit Cobbler

**SERVES 6 TO 8**

### TOPPING

1 cup all-purpose flour

½ cup firmly packed light brown sugar

¼ cup granulated sugar

½ cup old-fashioned rolled oats

3 tablespoons cold unsalted butter, cut into small cubes

2 tablespoons ground cinnamon

### FRUIT

½ cup unsalted butter

4 Honeycrisp apples, peeled, halved, cored, and sliced or chopped

1 cup firmly packed light brown sugar

½ cup water

½ cup dried cranberries

½ cup dried cherries

½ cup dried figs, stemmed and halved lengthwise

¼ cup fresh mint leaves, cut into thin strips

Vanilla ice cream for serving

Freshly cracked black pepper for serving (optional)

**For the topping:** Preheat the oven to 350°F. In a food processor, combine the flour, both sugars, and the oats and pulse a few times to mix. Scatter the butter cubes over the flour mixture and pulse just until the mixture resembles a coarse meal.

Sprinkle the mixture in a thin, even layer onto a rimmed baking sheet. Bake for 10 minutes. Remove from the oven, stir in the cinnamon, and then return to the oven. Bake until the mixture holds together in clumps and is beginning to brown, about 4 minutes longer. Remove from the oven. (The topping may be prepared up to 24 hours in advance; let cool completely, and store in an airtight container at room temperature. Just before serving, return the topping to the baking sheet and place in a preheated 350°F oven until warm, 6 to 8 minutes.)

**For the fruit:** While the topping is baking, in a large skillet, melt the butter over medium heat and cook just until it begins to brown and smells nutty, about 2 minutes. Add the apples and brown sugar and toss to combine. Add the water and all of the dried fruits and stir well. Bring to a gentle boil, adjust the heat to maintain a steady simmer, and cook until the apples begin to soften and the liquid in the pan is reduced to a syrup, 8 to 10 minutes. Remove from the heat and fold in the mint.

Transfer the fruit mixture to a large gratin dish and sprinkle the topping evenly over the surface. Alternatively, divide the fruit mixture evenly among 6 to 8 compote dishes and sprinkle an equal amount of the topping over each serving. Serve immediately with the ice cream. If you like, offer black pepper at the table to sprinkle on top.

"This is a lighter take on the traditional cobbler. Instead of baking the fruit for a half hour to crisp the topping, I bake the topping separately, and then gently sauté the fruit for just a few minutes to make a warm compote."

## CAT CORA

# A SOUTHERN THANKSGIVING

Cat treasures Thanksgiving because it's one of the few days when she and her wife turn off the cell phones, watch the parade on TV with their four kids over mugs of eggnog, and then spend the whole day cooking together. Her mixed southern and Greek heritage inspired her to create this menu that pays homage to the best of both worlds.

# Crisped Root Vegetable Salad
## with White Balsamic Syrup

"If you like the crispy coating on fried green tomatoes, you're going to love this southern-meets-Mediterranean salad topped with crispy fried root vegetables. It's definitely a special occasion thing with a lot going on—crunchy, sweet, tangy, and savory. Kids really go for it. And so do grown-ups."

**SERVES 6 TO 8**

1 cup white balsamic vinegar

2 tablespoons firmly packed light brown sugar

Vegetable oil for deep-frying

1 cup yellow cornmeal

1 cup all-purpose flour

1 teaspoon salt, plus more to season

½ teaspoon freshly ground black pepper, plus more to season

2 cups buttermilk

¼ head cauliflower, cut into bite-sized florets

1 small turnip, peeled and cut into ¼-inch-thick slices

1 carrot, peeled and cut on the diagonal into ¼-inch-thick slices

1 parsnip, peeled and cut on the diagonal into ¼-inch-thick slices

½ onion, quartered and separated

1 red beet, peeled and cut into ¼-inch-thick slices

4 cups arugula, mâche, or baby salad greens

4 teaspoons olive oil

In a small, heavy-bottomed saucepan, combine the vinegar and brown sugar and bring to a boil over high heat. Reduce the heat to medium and simmer until the mixture is reduced to the consistency of a syrup, 15 to 20 minutes. Remove from the heat and let cool to room temperature.

Pour the oil to a depth of 2 inches into a large Dutch oven, place over medium-high heat, and heat to 375°F. Line a large plate with several layers of paper towels. In a medium shallow bowl, stir together the cornmeal, flour, 1 teaspoon salt, and ½ teaspoon pepper. Pour the buttermilk into a second medium shallow bowl.

When the oil is ready, working in batches, dip the vegetables (cauliflower, turnip, carrot, parsnip, onion, and beet), one type at a time, into the buttermilk (dip the beets last because they will discolor it), and then into the cornmeal mixture, coating evenly. Using tongs, carefully place one type of breaded vegetable into the hot oil and fry, turning occasionally with the tongs or a slotted spoon, until golden brown on all sides, 3 to 4 minutes. Using the tongs or the slotted spoon, transfer the vegetable pieces to the towel-lined plate to drain, and season with salt while hot. Repeat with the remaining vegetables.

Place the arugula in a serving bowl. Drizzle with the olive oil, season with salt and pepper, and toss to coat evenly. Arrange the hot vegetables over and around the greens, and drizzle the whole salad with the white balsamic syrup. Or, dress the greens as directed, divide among individual plates, top with the vegetables, and drizzle each serving with the syrup. Serve right away.

# Slow-Roasted Bourbon Pork

**SERVES 6 TO 8**

2 tablespoons kosher salt

1 tablespoon freshly ground black pepper

1 bone-in pork shoulder, about 5 pounds

10 cloves garlic, peeled but left whole

10 fresh sage leaves

About 1 cup all-purpose flour

2 tablespoons extra virgin olive oil

Alma's Sweet-Hot Mustard (recipe follows)

½ cup firmly packed light brown sugar

4 or 5 dashes Worcestershire sauce

¼ cup bourbon

In a small bowl, mix together the salt and pepper, then rub the mixture over all sides of the pork. Using a sharp paring knife, make 5 slits on the leaner side of the pork, and stuff a garlic clove and sage leaf into each slit. Turn the pork over and repeat on the fattier side with the remaining 5 garlic cloves and 5 sage leaves. Wrap the pork in plastic wrap, place on a rimmed baking sheet, and refrigerate overnight.

Preheat the oven to 250°F.

Spread the flour on a large plate. Unwrap the pork and roll it around in the flour to coat all sides. Shake off any excess flour. In a large skillet, heat the olive oil over medium-high heat. Add the floured pork and cook, turning as needed, until golden brown on all sides (including the ends), about 15 minutes total.

Transfer the meat to a roasting pan just large enough to accommodate it. In a small bowl, stir together ½ cup of the mustard, the brown sugar, the Worcestershire sauce, and the bourbon, mixing until smooth. Smear the meat with about half of the mustard–brown sugar mixture, using enough to coat all sides evenly with a thin layer. Reserve the remaining mustard mixture.

Cover the roasting pan tightly with aluminum foil and place in the oven for 4 hours. Remove the foil and spoon the reserved mustard–brown sugar mixture over the top of the roast. Return to the oven, uncovered, and roast until the pork is completely tender and is falling from the bone, about 2 hours longer.

Transfer the meat to a cutting board and tent with foil to keep warm. Pour the pan juices into a 1-quart measuring pitcher and let stand for a few minutes to allow the fat to rise to the top. Skim off and discard the fat, taste the pan juices, and adjust the seasoning with salt and pepper if necessary. Keep the pan juices warm.

Slice the pork and arrange on a warmed platter. Pour the pan juices over the slices and serve right away. Pass the remaining mustard at the table.

# Alma's Sweet-Hot Mustard

**MAKES ABOUT 1½ CUPS**

½ cup Colman's dry mustard (about one 2-ounce can)

½ cup sugar

1 tablespoon all-purpose flour

½ teaspoon kosher salt

½ cup cider vinegar

1 tablespoon unsalted butter, melted

1 cup plus 2 tablespoons (9 ounces) prepared yellow mustard

In a small bowl, stir together the dry mustard, sugar, flour, and salt. Stir in the vinegar and melted butter, then fold in the prepared mustard until fully incorporated.

Cover tightly and refrigerate for at least 24 hours to allow the dry mustard to release its full heat and meld with the rest of the ingredients before using. The mustard will keep for up to 2 weeks in the refrigerator.

"This recipe goes all the way back to my great-grandmother. The bourbon gives a nod to the South, but the secret ingredient is my grandmother Alma's homemade mustard."

# Garlic Mashed Potatoes

"I am my father's daughter, and he lives by the rule that occasionally you pull out all the stops and eat exactly what your heart desires—like these heavenly mashed potatoes. They're extra creamy and totally irresistible."

**SERVES 6 TO 8**

3 teaspoons kosher salt

4 large baking potatoes, about 4 pounds total weight

8 tablespoons unsalted butter

3 cloves garlic, minced

⅔ cup whole milk

⅔ cup heavy cream

Freshly ground black pepper

Fill a large pot three-fourths full of water and bring to a boil over high heat. Add 2 teaspoons of the salt. While the water is heating, peel the potatoes and cut into 1-inch cubes.

Add the potatoes to the boiling water and cook until fork-tender, 10 to 12 minutes.

While the potatoes are cooking, in a skillet, melt 6 tablespoons of the butter over low heat; reserve the remaining 2 tablespoons butter at room temperature. When the butter is melted, add the garlic and cook until it starts to color, 3 to 4 minutes. Take care not to burn the butter. Remove from the heat and set aside.

When the potatoes are ready, drain them in a colander and return them to the pot off the heat; the residual heat from the cooking pot will help to evaporate the excess water, which will make your potatoes light and fluffy. Pass the potatoes through a ricer held over a bowl, or mash them in the bowl with a potato masher. Gradually add the milk and cream, stirring with a rubber spatula or wooden spoon until thoroughly combined. Stir in the butter and garlic mixture and season with the remaining 1 teaspoon salt.

Transfer the potatoes to a warmed serving bowl or platter. Cut the reserved 2 tablespoons butter into bits and dot them over the surface of the potatoes. Serve right away. Pass the pepper mill at the table.

# Sautéed Greens with Meyer Lemon and Garlic

"If you lived on an island in Greece, you'd hike to the top of the hill to pick some wild greens and this is how you'd cook them. Meanwhile, you can hike over to the farmer's market and pick out some nice chard or kale, or, depending on the season, try arugula, dandelion, chicory, mustard, or broccoli rabe."

**SERVES 6 TO 8**

4 pounds Swiss chard or kale, tough stems removed and leaves coarsely chopped

2 tablespoons kosher salt, plus more to season

½ cup extra virgin olive oil

6 cloves garlic, thinly sliced

6 to 8 tablespoons fresh Meyer lemon juice (from 3 to 4 lemons)

Freshly cracked black pepper

Bring a large pot three-fourths full of water to a boil over high heat. Add the greens and the 2 tablespoons salt. Bring the water back to a gentle boil, cover the pot partially, and cook until the greens are tender, 4 to 5 minutes.

Place a large colander in the sink. Drain the greens in the colander and let them sit to drain and cool for about 10 minutes. Once the greens are cool enough to handle, squeeze all the excess moisture from them with your hands. (The recipe can be completed up to this point several hours in advance. Set the greens aside at room temperature for up to 2 hours, or refrigerate if longer.)

In a large sauté pan, heat the olive oil over medium-high heat until it shimmers. Add the garlic and cook, stirring, until it begins to brown, 1 to 2 minutes. Add the greens and sauté until heated through, 2 to 3 minutes. Remove from the heat, add half of the lemon juice, season to taste with salt and pepper, and toss well.

Taste again and adjust the seasoning with more lemon juice, salt, and pepper if needed. Transfer to a warmed serving bowl or platter and serve right away.

# VaLee's White Chocolate Pecan Pie

**SERVES 12**

1 pie crust for a 9-inch pie, homemade or store-bought

2 cups pecan halves

1⅓ cups white chocolate chips or vanilla-flavored chips

3 large eggs

¾ cup firmly packed light brown sugar

¾ cup light corn syrup

3 tablespoons all-purpose flour

Nonstick cooking spray, if needed

Whipped cream or ice cream for serving (optional)

Preheat the oven to 400°F.

Roll out the pie dough and use to line a 9-inch pie pan. Layer the pecans and white chocolate chips on the bottom of the pie shell.

In a medium bowl, whisk the eggs until blended. Whisk in the brown sugar, corn syrup, and flour until thoroughly combined. Carefully pour the egg mixture over the nuts and white chocolate chips, trying not to dislodge them.

Bake the pie until the crust is golden brown and the filling is set in the center, 35 to 40 minutes. Check after about 25 minutes, and if the pie is browning too quickly, spray a piece of aluminum foil on one side with nonstick cooking spray and place it, sprayed side down, over the pie, covering it loosely. Transfer the pie to a wire rack and let cool completely, about 2 hours.

Eat right away, or cover and store in the refrigerator for up to 3 days. The pie is best at room temperature, but it can also be served warm or chilled. Top each slice with a dollop of whipped cream, if desired.

"My mom, VaLee, makes this classic pie with a sweet little twist: a layer of white chocolate chips nestled in with the pecans."

## NANCY SILVERTON
# LEFTOVERS FOR LUNCH

Who doesn't look forward to that day-after lunch? And who better to ask for creative ideas than Nancy Silverton, who literally wrote the book on sandwiches? "Thanksgiving is the meal that keeps on giving," she says. "And it's always nice to have simple ways to turn the leftovers into something easy but just that little bit different."

# Sicilian Waldorf Turkey Salad Sandwich

"One of the cooks at Campanile came up with this Italian-inspired Waldorf made with currants and pine nuts, and I like it just as much as the original grape-and-walnut version. It's equally good with leftover turkey or chicken, on a sandwich or as a salad over greens."

**MAKES 4 SANDWICHES**

### MUSTARD MAYONNAISE

1 cup mayonnaise

2 tablespoons extra virgin olive oil

1½ teaspoons Dijon mustard, or more to taste

1 tablespoon fresh lemon juice, or more to taste

Kosher salt

½ cup pine nuts

1½ pounds roasted turkey, meat shredded and skin and bones discarded (3 to 4 cups)

1 celery stalk, peeled and cut into ¼-inch dice

½ cup dried currants

¼ cup finely chopped fresh flat-leaf parsley

2 to 3 tablespoons fresh lemon juice

Kosher salt and freshly cracked black pepper

8 slices La Brea Bakery Whole Grain Loaf, about ½ inch thick

For the mustard mayonnaise: In a small bowl, stir together the mayonnaise, olive oil, mustard, lemon juice, and a pinch of salt. Taste and adjust the seasoning with more lemon juice, mustard, and/or salt if needed. Set aside.

Preheat the oven to 325°F.

Spread the pine nuts on a rimmed baking sheet, place in the oven, and toast, shaking the pan occasionally, until lightly browned, about 8 minutes. Remove from the oven and let cool.

In large bowl, mix together the turkey and ½ to ¾ cup of the mayonnaise to taste. Add the toasted pine nuts, celery, currants, parsley, and 2 tablespoons of the lemon juice and mix to combine evenly. Add more mayonnaise if needed to coat the turkey well. Season with salt and pepper, then taste and adjust with more lemon juice if needed.

Spread one side of half of the bread slices with 1 to 2 tablespoons of the mayonnaise. Divide the turkey salad evenly among the mayonnaise-topped bread slices. Top each sandwich with a second slice of bread, then cut the sandwiches in half on the diagonal to serve.

# Spicy Turkey Sandwich with Chipotle Mayonnaise

**MAKES 4 SANDWICHES**

**CHIPOTLE MAYONNAISE**

1 cup mayonnaise

¼ cup finely chopped fresh cilantro

2 tablespoons extra virgin olive oil

2 tablespoons fresh lemon juice, or more to taste

4 large cloves garlic, grated or minced (about 1 tablespoon), or more to taste

1½ teaspoons puréed *chipotle chiles en adobo*, or more to taste

1 teaspoon kosher salt, or more to taste

1 cup shredded iceberg lettuce

8 slices La Brea Bakery Country White Sourdough Loaf, ¼ inch thick

1½ pounds roasted turkey, meat sliced or shredded and skin and bones discarded (3 to 4 cups)

8 large tomato slices

**For the chipotle mayonnaise:** In a small bowl, stir together the mayonnaise, cilantro, olive oil, lemon juice, garlic, puréed chiles, and salt and mix well. Taste and adjust the seasoning with more lemon juice, garlic, puréed chile, and/or salt if needed. You should have a generous 1 cup. Use immediately, or cover and refrigerate for up to 3 days before using.

**To assemble the sandwiches:** In a small bowl, toss together the lettuce and ½ cup of the mayonnaise. Spread one side of each bread slice with 1 teaspoon of the mayonnaise. (Cover and refrigerate the remaining mayonnaise for another use.) Evenly divide the turkey among 4 of the bread slices. Top each turkey portion with 2 tomato slices and then with one-fourth of the lettuce-mayonnaise mixture. Top each sandwich with a second slice of bread, mayonnaise side down. Cut in half on the diagonal to serve.

# Grilled Sage Cheddar and Turkey Sandwich with Leeks and Celery

**MAKES 4 SANDWICHES**

2 celery stalks

1 leek

3 tablespoons unsalted butter, plus 2 tablespoons softened

Kosher salt and freshly ground black pepper

8 slices La Brea Bakery French Loaf or Country White Sourdough Loaf, ½ inch thick

12 ounces Bravo Farms sage Cheddar cheese, shredded, or 12 ounces white Cheddar cheese, shredded and tossed with 1 to 2 tablespoons chopped fresh sage

8 ounces roasted turkey breast, sliced or coarsely shredded

8 fresh sage leaves

Using a vegetable peeler, peel each celery stalk, then cut off the broad white end and discard or reserve for another use. Cut the green part crosswise into ⅛-inch-thick slices. Cut off and discard the dark green tops of the leek, then slice the white and light green parts in half lengthwise. Cut crosswise into 2-inch-long pieces, then cut each piece lengthwise into julienne.

In a small pan, melt the 3 tablespoons butter over medium-low heat. Add the celery, season with salt and pepper, cover, and cook until barely tender, about 3 minutes. Add the leek to the celery, stir well, re-cover, and cook until the celery and leek are tender but have not colored, 7 to 8 minutes. Remove from the heat and set aside.

**To assemble the sandwiches:** Lightly spread the bread slices on one side with the softened butter. Place half of the bread slices, buttered side down, on a work surface and evenly sprinkle ½ cup of the Cheddar on each slice. Divide the turkey evenly among the sandwiches, layering it on top of the cheese, then divide the celery mixture evenly among the sandwiches, spreading it over turkey. Sprinkle the remaining Cheddar over the celery mixture, dividing it evenly among the sandwiches. Top with the remaining bread slices, buttered side up. Place 2 sage leaves on the top slice of each sandwich before grilling.

Preheat a skillet over medium-high heat, or preheat a panini grill medium-hot. Cook the sandwiches in the skillet or the grill until golden brown and the cheese has melted, 4 to 5 minutes. If using a skillet, turn the sandwiches over halfway through cooking.

Cut the sandwiches in half on the diagonal and serve hot.

"Chipotle mayo takes leftover turkey to a whole new place flavorwise. Tossing the shredded lettuce in some of the mayo makes every bite moist and juicy."

"This toasted sandwich, gives you all the familiar flavors of turkey and stuffing in every bite."

"Hold the mayo and try this enlightened turkey salad, with a light, zingy vinaigrette, plenty of flavorful fresh greens, the toasty crunch of almonds, and a bit of salty-creamy feta. It's a great choice for feeding a post-Thanksgiving crowd."

# Radicchio, Arugula, and Frisée Salad
## with Roasted Turkey, Feta, and Almonds

**SERVES 4**

### MUSTARD VINAIGRETTE

2 tablespoons minced shallots

2 tablespoons fresh lemon juice

1½ teaspoons Champagne vinegar

¼ cup extra virgin olive oil

½ teaspoon kosher salt

¼ teaspoon freshly ground black pepper

⅓ cup whole-grain Dijon mustard

¾ cup raw almonds

½ teaspoon olive oil

Fine sea salt

¾ cup cubed roasted turkey breast (¾-inch cubes)

4 cups torn radicchio, or 4 heads Belgian endive, leaves separated, cut into ½-inch pieces

4 cups frisée, torn if leaves are large

4 cups arugula

½ lemon

10 ounces feta cheese

For the mustard vinaigrette: In a small bowl, combine the shallots, lemon juice, and vinegar and set aside for 5 to 10 minutes to marinate the shallots. Add the olive oil in a slow, steady stream, whisking constantly to emulsify. Whisk in the salt and pepper, then whisk in the mustard. Taste and adjust the seasoning with salt if needed. You should have about ¾ cup. Use immediately, or transfer to an airtight container and refrigerate for up to 3 days.

For the salad: Preheat the oven to 325°F. Spread the almonds on a rimmed baking sheet, place in the oven, and toast, shaking the pan occasionally, until the nuts take on color and are fragrant, 15 to 20 minutes. Remove from the oven, drizzle with the olive oil, sprinkle with the salt, and toss to coat. Let the almonds cool slightly, then coarsely chop and set aside.

Place the turkey in a large bowl. Add a few tablespoons of the vinaigrette and toss to coat. Allow the turkey to "marinate" for a few minutes.

Add the radicchio, frisée, and arugula to the bowl with the turkey. Drizzle ½ cup of the mustard vinaigrette over the salad and toss gently with your hands to coat the leaves evenly. Sprinkle with salt and again toss gently with your hands to distribute the salt evenly. Taste for seasoning and add more vinaigrette, a squeeze of lemon juice, or salt if needed. Reserve any remaining vinaigrette for another use.

Pile the salad on a large platter or divide among individual plates. Crumble the feta over the top and serve right away.

# Pumpkin Tart

*"This is my kind of pumpkin pie—a tart made with just a hint of pumpkin and plenty of cream."*

**SERVES 8**

### PASTRY SHELL

**1 cup plus 6 tablespoons unbleached pastry flour or all-purpose flour**

**¼ cup sugar**

**½ cup unsalted butter, frozen and cubed**

**1 extra-large egg yolk**

**2 tablespoons heavy cream**

### FILLING

**1½ cups heavy cream**

**½ teaspoon pumkin pie spice**

**⅛ teaspoon salt**

**5 large egg yolks**

**6 tablespoons sugar**

**½ cup canned pumpkin purée**

**Whipped cream for serving**

**For the pastry shell:** In a food processor, combine the flour and sugar and pulse a few times to mix well. Scatter the butter over the top and pulse until the mixture is the consistency of a fine meal. In a small bowl, whisk together the egg yolk and cream. Add to the processor and pulse a few times until the dough barely comes together.

Alternatively, in a stand mixer fitted with the paddle attachment, combine the flour and sugar and mix on low speed until combined. Scatter the butter over the top and mix on low speed until the mixture is the consistency of a fine meal. Add the egg yolk–cream mixture to the mixer and mix on low speed until the dough barely comes together.

Turn the dough out onto a lightly floured work surface. Dip the heel of your hand in flour and, working with a single small section at a time, smear the dough away from you to blend the ingredients together. When all of the dough is blended, flatten the dough into a disk, wrap in plastic wrap, and chill until firm, at least 2 hours.

Place a 10¼-inch tart ring on a rimmed baking sheet. On a lightly floured work surface, roll out the dough into a 12-inch circle. Loosely drape the dough circle over the tart ring, then ease the pastry into place, pressing it firmly but gently against the sides and bottom and allowing the excess dough to extend over the rim. Roll the rolling pin over the top of the tart ring to cut off the excess pastry. Refrigerate for 20 minutes to chill. Reserve the pastry trimmings for patching. Meanwhile, preheat the oven to 350°F.

Line the bottom and sides of the chilled tart shell with round coffee filters or parchment paper, and fill the shell with pie weights or raw rice, making sure you fill to the edges. Bake until the pastry is golden brown, about 25 minutes. Remove from the oven and leave the oven set at 350°F. Let the pastry shell cool for a few minutes on a rack. Then, using a large spoon, remove the weights and carefully peel off the coffee filters or parchment. If the bottom of the pastry is not uniformly browned, return it unlined to the oven for a few minutes until evenly colored, then let cool completely before filling.

Before you fill the shell, check for any cracks. If you find some, smear a small amount of raw dough (from trimming the edges) over the cracks to repair them.

**For the filling:** Once the pastry shell is in the oven, begin making the filling. In a saucepan, combine the cream, pumpkin pie spice, and salt. Bring to a boil over high heat. Meanwhile, in a small bowl, whisk together the egg yolks and sugar until smooth.

When the cream begins to boil, remove from the heat. Slowly whisk about half of the hot cream into the egg yolk mixture, then whisk the egg yolk–cream mixture into the cream remaining in the pan. Return the pan to low heat and cook, stirring constantly, until the custard coats the back of a spoon, 1 to 2 minutes.

Using a fine-mesh sieve, strain the custard into a medium bowl. Stir in the pumpkin and let the filling cool while the crust bakes. Skim off any foam that develops on the surface of the custard as it cools.

**To assemble and bake the tart:** Slowly pour the prepared pumpkin custard into the center of the pastry shell, and then carefully transfer the baking sheet to the oven. Bake until the filling is set, 25 to 30 minutes. Let the tart cool completely on a rack.

Lift off the tart ring, then, using a wide metal spatula, carefully transfer the tart to a serving plate. Cut the tart into wedges and top each serving with a dollop of whipped cream.

# HOLIDAY

# FRIENDS AND FAMILY COOKIE EXCHANGE

For a fun DIY holiday gathering, invite friends over for a cookie exchange. Depending on the size of your kitchen, you can ask people to bring finished cookies, dough, or raw ingredients. Have plenty of tins, boxes, gift bags, tags, and ribbons on hand for packing every-thing up. Here are adaptations of some signature treats from Macy's restaurants nationwide to inspire you.

# Chocolate Pecan Pie Bars *Frontera Fresco*

These bars from Rick Bayless are perfect for a buffet or party. Instead of pastry, they feature an easy crust of bread crumbs and crunchy Mexican chocolate, and the rich, not-too-sweet filling gets the gooey factor just right.

**MAKES 24 BARS**

2½ cups (about 10 ounces) pecan halves

1 cup (about 6 ounces) finely chopped Mexican chocolate (such as the widely available Ibarra brand)

6 ounces (6 to 8 slices) fresh white bread (preferably cakey sandwich bread like Pepperidge Farm brand), torn into large pieces

1 cup (8 ounces) melted butter, plus more for coating the pan

Generous ¾ teaspoon salt

5 ounces semisweet or bittersweet chocolate, chopped into pieces not larger than ¼ inch

3 tablespoons all-purpose flour

4 large eggs

1 cup firmly packed dark brown sugar

1 cup corn syrup, preferably dark (or use a mixture of corn syrup and molasses, sorghum, Steen's cane syrup, or almost any other rich-flavored syrup on the market)

2 teaspoons pure vanilla extract

Confectioners' sugar for dusting

Preheat the oven to 325°F degrees. Spread the pecans on a rimmed baking sheet, place in the oven, and bake until richly browned and toasty smelling, about 10 minutes. Remove from the oven and let cool.

Scoop the cooled nuts into a food processor and pulse until coarsely chopped. Remove about 1½ cups of the nuts and put them in a large bowl to use in the filling.

Add ½ cup of the Mexican chocolate to the nuts in the food processor and pulse to mix. Add the bread and process until everything is fairly fine crumbs. Add ⅓ cup of the melted butter and ¼ teaspoon of the salt and process just to moisten everything. (If you lack a food processor, you can chop each item separately with any other appliance or gadget you deem appropriate, then combine them in a bowl with the melted butter and salt.)

Liberally butter a 9-by-13-inch baking pan. Turn the crumb crust mixture into the pan and pat it evenly over the bottom. Refrigerate the crust while you make the filling.

Add the remaining ½ cup Mexican chocolate, the chopped semisweet chocolate, and the flour to the bowl with the reserved pecans. In the food processor (you don't even need to clean it), combine the eggs and brown sugar and process until well combined. Add the corn syrup, pulse a couple of times, and add the remaining ⅔ cup melted butter, the remaining ½ teaspoon salt, and the vanilla. Process to combine thoroughly, then pour it over the pecan-chocolate mixture in the bowl and stir well. Scrape the filling into your crust-lined pan and spread evenly.

Bake until the bars have pulled away slightly from the sides of the pan, 40 to 50 minutes. Transfer the pan to a rack and let cool to room temperature before cutting. Cut into 2-inch squares, then dust with confectioners' sugar and arrange on an attractive platter to serve.

**RICK'S TIPS:** To make removing the bars from the pan easy, line the pan with a carefully flattened piece of heavy-duty foil and butter the foil, then use the foil to lift out the finished bars. The baked sheet of bars will be easier to cut if you chill it first.

# Star Cookies *Macy's Marketplace*

This recipe is a holiday essential: a versatile butter cookie dough and a simple icing that you can turn into creative holiday cookies of all shapes and sizes. You can use a variety of cookie cutters and color the icing with food coloring to make everything from trees, reindeer, and Santa to edible ornaments. Use melted chocolate, as directed, to outline and add details.

## MAKES ABOUT 3 DOZEN COOKIES

¾ cup granulated sugar

1½ cups unsalted butter, at room temperature, plus more for the baking sheet

1 large egg

¼ teaspoon pure vanilla extract

½ teaspoon baking powder

3½ cups all-purpose flour

### ICING

6 cups confectioners' sugar

6 to 9 tablespoons whole milk

¾ teaspoon pure vanilla extract

1½ teaspoons liquid red food coloring

6 ounces semisweet chocolate, chopped

In the bowl of a stand mixer fitted with the paddle attachment, combine the granulated sugar and butter and beat on medium speed until light and fluffy, 2 to 3 minutes. Add the egg, vanilla, and baking powder and beat until incorporated. On low speed, add the flour and mix just until the dough starts to come together.

Remove the dough from the mixer and shape into a large, flat disk, kneading it briefly on a lightly floured work surface if necessary to bring it together. Wrap the disk in plastic wrap and refrigerate for at least 1 hour or up to 2 hours.

Preheat the oven to 350°F. Butter 2 large baking sheets.

On a lightly floured work surface, roll out the dough ¼ inch thick. Using a 3½-inch star-shaped cookie cutter, cut out stars. Transfer the stars to a prepared baking sheet, spacing them about 1 inch apart. Gather up the scraps, roll out again, and cut out more stars. You can reroll any scraps once more if necessary.

Bake the cookies, 1 sheet at a time, until lightly golden, 15 to 20 minutes. Let cool completely on the pan on a rack.

**For the icing:** In a bowl, combine the confectioners' sugar, 6 tablespoons of the milk, the vanilla, and the food coloring and stir until smooth. If the icing is too thick to spread, add up to 3 tablespoons milk, a little at a time, until it is smooth and pourable but still thick enough to coat. Transfer the icing to a measuring cup with a spout.

Set a wire rack over a piece of waxed paper or parchment paper. Place the cooled cookies on the rack. Pour about 2 tablespoons of the icing onto each cookie, and then use a metal icing spatula to spread it evenly to the points of the star. You may not need all of the icing. Let the cookies stand for 1 hour to set the icing.

Put the chocolate in a heatproof bowl. Place over (not touching) barely simmering water in a saucepan and heat, stirring often, until melted and smooth, 5 to 7 minutes. Remove the bowl from the saucepan and let the chocolate cool until no longer hot but still fluid.

Transfer the chocolate to a squeeze bottle, a resealable plastic bag, or a pastry bag fitted with a ¹⁄₁₆-inch round tip. If using a plastic bag, snip off a small piece of a lower corner. Using the bottle, plastic bag, or pastry bag, pipe a narrow chocolate border around the edge of each star. Let stand for 1 to 2 hours to set the chocolate.

The cookies may be stored in an airtight container at room temperature for up to 3 days.

Look for world-famous Frango™ Chocolates at your local Macy's or at macys.com. Besides being the perfect holiday gift, they contain everything you need to create professional-looking chocolate-coated treats.

# Frango-Dipped Treats *Macy's Marketplace*

### Chocolate Pretzels

Sweet-salty never tasted better. Use this same technique for dipping candy canes.

MAKES 24 PRETZELS

**30 Frango Chocolates (Mint, Dark Mint, Double Chocolate, or Dark Chocolate)**

**24 pretzel rods**

**Chocolate sprinkles, finely chopped Frango Chocolates, and/or finely chopped toasted nuts for garnish**

**To melt the Frango Chocolates:** You can melt the chocolates in a microwave or a double boiler. To use a microwave, put the chocolates in a microwave-safe bowl and microwave at half power for about 2 minutes, let stand briefly, then stir. Microwave for additional 15-second increments as needed, stirring after each increment, just until the chocolate is melted.

To use a double boiler, put the chocolates in the top pan and set it over (not touching) barely simmering water in the bottom pan. Or, use a heatproof bowl that fits snugly in the rim of a saucepan. Stir the chocolate occasionally and remove it from the heat as soon as it is melted. Avoid heating the chocolate any longer than necessary, and don't let water splash into it, which can cause it to seize (form clumps and become grainy).

Line a baking sheet with waxed paper. Put the chocolate in a tall, narrow drinking glass. Dip a pretzel about one-third of the way into the chocolate, allowing the excess chocolate to drip back into the glass. Place on the prepared baking sheet. Repeat with the remaining pretzels. As the chocolate is depleted, you may need to tilt the glass to coat the last few pretzels.

While the chocolate is still warm, sprinkle the chosen garnish(es) on the pretzels. Let stand until the chocolate has hardened, about 4 hours. The pretzels will keep in an airtight container at room temperature for a week or more

### Frango Mangoes

These easy-to-make candies are elegant enough to give as a gift or to serve with coffee and after-dinner drinks at a holiday meal. You can also use other dried fruits, such as apricots or pears, or cookies, like biscotti or amaretti.

MAKES 24 CANDIES

**15 Frango Chocolates (Double Chocolate or Dark Chocolate)**

**24 pieces dried mango (about 7 ounces)**

**¼ cup finely chopped salted roasted pistachios**

Melt the Frango Chocolates as directed in Chocolate Pretzels (above).

Line a baking sheet with waxed paper. Put the chocolate in a coffee cup. Dip a mango piece about halfway into the chocolate, allowing the excess chocolate to drip back into the cup. Place on the prepared baking sheet. Repeat with the remaining mango pieces. As the chocolate is depleted, you may need to tilt the cup to coat the last few mango pieces.

While the chocolate is still warm, sprinkle with the pistachios. Let stand until the chocolate has hardened, about 4 hours. The mango pieces will keep in an airtight container at room temperature for up to 1 week.

### White Chocolate Drizzle

Use this simple method to give any Frango-dipped confection a professional-looking finish.

MAKES ENOUGH TO GARNISH ABOUT 24 TREATS

**One 3½-ounce bar white chocolate, chopped**

Put the chocolate in a small heatproof bowl, place over (not touching) barely simmering water in a saucepan, and heat, stirring often, until melted and smooth. Remove the bowl from the saucepan. Or, put the chocolate in a microwave-safe bowl and microwave at half power for about 1 minute, let stand briefly, then stir. Microwave for additional 15-second increments as needed, stirring after each increment, just until the chocolate is melted.

Using a rapid back-and-forth motion, drizzle the chocolate from the tip of a spoon over the confection you want to decorate. (You can practice over waxed paper until you achieve attractive, uniform lines of chocolate, then scoop up the chocolate and return it to the bowl or pan.) Let stand until the chocolate has hardened, about 4 hours.

# Frango-Filled Shortbread Cookies *Macy's Marketplace*

Frango Chocolates are the simple secret to the soft chocolate center of these delicate shortbread cookies.

**MAKES ABOUT 3 DOZEN COOKIES**

1 cup unsalted butter, at room temperature

½ cup confectioners' sugar, plus more for rolling

2 cups cake flour

1 teaspoon pure vanilla extract

Pinch of salt

1 cup finely chopped pecans

18 Frango Mint Chocolates, halved crosswise

In a stand mixer fitted with the paddle attachment, or in a bowl with a hand-held mixer, combine the butter and confectioners' sugar and beat on medium-high speed until pale yellow and fluffy, about 1 minute. Using a wooden spoon, stir in the flour, vanilla, and salt until fully incorporated. Stir in the pecans. Cover the bowl with plastic wrap and refrigerate until the dough is firm, about 1 hour.

Position a rack in the center and in the upper third of the oven and preheat to 350°F. Have ready 2 ungreased baking sheets.

Scoop out a level tablespoon of dough and shape it around a chocolate half, enclosing the chocolate completely. Roll the dough between your palms to form a ball. Repeat with the remaining dough and chocolates. As the cookies are shaped, arrange them on the baking sheets, spacing them about 1 inch apart.

Bake the cookies, switching the pans between the racks and rotating them 180 degrees about halfway through the baking time, until golden brown, 18 to 20 minutes.

Meanwhile, sift confectioners' sugar into a small bowl. When the cookies are ready, remove them from the oven, let them cool on the pans on racks just until they can be handled, and then roll them in the sugar, coating them well. Put the coated cookies on the racks and let cool completely. The cookies may be stored in an airtight container at room temperature for up to 1 week.

# Peanutters *CCQ*

Cat Cora's Macy's eatery, known as CCQ (that's short for Cat Cora's Que), features these satisfyingly simple peanut butter cookies, loaded with roasted peanuts and chocolate chips.

**MAKES ABOUT 3 DOZEN COOKIES**

Nonstick cooking spray (optional)

2¼ cups all-purpose flour

1 teaspoon baking soda

1 teaspoon salt

¾ cup unsalted butter, at warm room temperature

¼ cup peanut butter (preferably salted crunchy)

¾ cup granulated sugar

¾ cup firmly packed dark brown sugar

1 teaspoon pure vanilla extract

2 large eggs

1½ cups chocolate chips (preferably ¾ cup each milk chocolate and semisweet chocolate)

1 cup salted cocktail peanuts, coarsely chopped

Position a rack in the center and in the upper third of the oven and preheat to 350°F. Spray 2 baking sheets with cooking spray or line with parchment paper.

In a medium bowl, stir together the flour, baking soda, and salt. Set aside.

In a stand mixer fitted with the paddle attachment, or in a bowl with a handheld mixer, combine the butter, peanut butter, granulated sugar, brown sugar, and vanilla extract and beat on medium-high speed until creamy, about 3 minutes. Add the eggs one at a time, beating well after each addition. On low speed, add the flour mixture in two batches, beating after each addition just until combined. With a wooden spoon, stir in the chocolate chips and peanuts.

Drop the dough by rounded teaspoons onto the prepared pans, spacing them about 2 inches apart.

Bake the cookies, switching the pans between the racks and rotating them 180 degrees about halfway through the baking time, until lightly golden, 11 to 12 minutes. Remove from the oven and let cool on the pans on racks for 1 to 2 minutes, then transfer the cookies to the racks and let cool completely. The cookies may be stored in an airtight container at room temperature for up to 4 days.

# Thumbprint Cookies *adapted from Macy's Arcade Bakery and Café, Pittsburg*

**MAKES ABOUT 5 DOZEN COOKIES**

1⅓ cups granulated sugar

¾ teaspoon salt

2 cups solid vegetable shortening, at room temperature

1½ cups butter, at room temperature

1 large egg

½ teaspoon pure vanilla extract

½ teaspoon pure rum extract

8¼ cups cake flour

Decorating sugar in various colors, rainbow sprinkles, and/or finely chopped nuts

Position a rack in the center and in the upper third of the oven and preheat to 375°F. Have ready 2 ungreased baking sheets.

In a stand mixer fitted with the paddle attachment, combine the granulated sugar, salt, shortening, and butter and beat on medium speed until light and fluffy, 2 to 3 minutes. Add the egg and the vanilla and rum extracts and beat until incorporated. On low speed, add the flour and mix just until the dough comes together. (If it doesn't look like all of the flour will fit into the bowl of your mixer, scoop the butter-shortening mixture out into a large bowl and, using a rubber spatula, gently fold in the flour just until combined.)

Put the decorating sugars, sprinkles and/or nuts in separate bowls. To shape each cookie, scoop up a heaping tablespoon of the dough, or use a 1-ounce scoop, and roll between you palms into a ball. As the balls are shaped, roll them in the decorating sugar, sprinkles, or nuts, coating them evenly on all sides, and place them on a baking sheet, spacing them 2 inches apart. Using your thumb, make a shallow indentation in the center of each cookie.

Bake the cookies, switching the pans between the racks and rotating them 180 degrees about halfway through the baking time, until a light golden brown, 18 to 20 minutes.

Remove from the oven, transfer the cookies to a rack, and let cool completely. The cookies may be stored in an airtight container at room temperature for up to 5 days.

These easy thumbprint cookies are a good choice for baking with kids. Get out the sprinkles, chopped nuts, and colored sugars and let 'em roll.

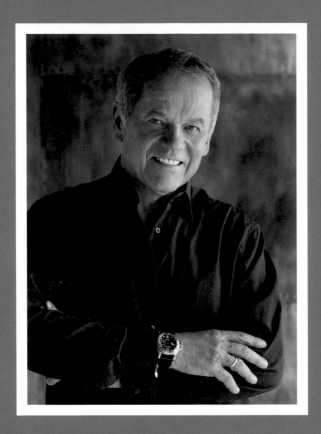

# WOLFGANG PUCK
# HOLIDAY
# BRUNCH

Wolfgang believes every holiday meal should have special touches that turn familiar ingredients and preparations into something extraordinary. "That doesn't mean the recipes need to be more complicated or difficult to make," he says. "Even just a hint of sweet spice or an unexpected but still easy-to-find ingredient can make a big difference."

# Cantaloupe Salad with Prosciutto and Ice Wine Dressing

"Melon and prosciutto are classic Italian antipasto partners. Here, I've made them the centerpiece of a simple, flavorful holiday salad, lightly coated with a sweet-and-tangy dressing."

**SERVES 8**

2 ripe cantaloupes

¼ cup ice wine *(Eiswein)* or other sweet white dessert wine

2 tablespoons extra virgin olive oil

2 teaspoons Champagne vinegar

1 tablespoon balsamic vinegar (preferably aged)

Salt and freshly ground black pepper

8 thin slices prosciutto

4 cups loosely packed baby mâche or butter lettuce leaves

With a sharp knife, cut each cantaloupe in half through the stem end. Using a spoon, scoop out and discard the seeds and strings from each half. Then, with a large, sharp knife, cut each melon half into slices about ¼ inch thick. With a paring knife, neatly cut away the rind and any hard, pale, or green flesh from each slice, leaving just the ripe orange fruit. Arrange the cantaloupe slices in a large, shallow dish.

**For the ice wine dressing:** In a small bowl, stir together the wine, olive oil, Champagne vinegar, and balsamic vinegar and season with salt and pepper. Drizzle 1½ tablespoons of the dressing over the cantaloupe slices and turn the slices to coat evenly. (At this point, the dish may be covered and refrigerated for no more than 1 hour before continuing.)

Divide the cantaloupe slices evenly among individual serving plates. Drape 1 prosciutto slice over the cantaloupe slices on each plate. Put the mâche leaves in the shallow dish you used for dressing the cantaloupe slices, add the remaining dressing, and toss until the leaves are evenly coated. Arrange the mâche attractively on each plate, dividing it evenly. Serve immediately.

"Everyone enjoys finding a plate of freshly baked muffins on a brunch table. A simple glaze adds a special holiday touch."

# Orange and Chocolate–Cinnamon Swirl Muffins

**MAKES 12 MUFFINS**

1½ cups all-purpose flour

½ cup sugar

2 teaspoons baking powder

½ teaspoon salt

1 large cage-free egg

½ cup buttermilk

½ cup orange juice

½ cup unsalted butter, melted,
   or ½ cup vegetable oil

1 teaspoon pure vanilla extract

1½ teaspoons grated orange zest

2 tablespoons unsweetened cocoa
   powder

½ cup milk chocolate chips

1 teaspoon ground cinnamon

½ cup thin-shred orange marmalade

Preheat the oven to 375°F. Line 12 standard (4-ounce) muffin-tin cups with paper liners.

**For the batter:** In a large bowl, sift together the flour, sugar, baking powder, and salt. In a separate medium bowl, whisk together the egg, buttermilk, orange juice, melted butter, vanilla, and orange zest. Pour the egg mixture into the bowl of dry ingredients. With a fork or whisk, stir the mixtures together just until you have a uniformly moist batter. Do not overstir; it is okay if a few streaks of flour remain.

Pour or spoon half of the batter (about 1½ cups) into another medium bowl. Stir all of the cocoa powder and half of the chocolate chips into the batter in the first bowl. Stir the remaining chocolate chips and all of the cinnamon into the second bowl.

**To fill the muffin cups and bake:** Adding 1 tablespoonful at a time, and alternating the spoonfuls between the 2 bowls to produce a swirled effect, transfer the batters to the prepared muffin cups, filling each cup about two-thirds full.

Place the muffins in the oven and bake for 12 minutes. Rotate the muffin tin 180 degrees and continue to bake until a long wooden toothpick or a cake tester inserted into the center of a muffin comes out clean, 5 to 8 minutes longer. Let cool on a rack in the pan for about 10 minutes, then remove and place on a platter.

Put the marmalade in a microwave-safe bowl and microwave, uncovered, on full power for about 30 seconds until slightly fluid, stopping to stir once after about 15 seconds and adding a few more seconds to the time if necessary. Spoon a little marmalade evenly over the top of each warm muffin and let stand for a few minutes to allow the glaze to set before serving.

# Crab Cakes "Benedict"

"Your guests will be surprised and delighted to find that plump, sweet crab cakes have replaced the usual Canadian bacon in this version of the brunch classic. I also leave out the hollandaise, which seems unnecessary with the moist, flavorful crab cakes. Cooking the eggs sunny-side up instead of poaching them is quicker and less fussy. This makes twelve portions, so your hungrier guests can enjoy two muffin halves instead of one."

**MAKES 12**

**CRAB CAKES**

2 tablespoons extra virgin olive oil

½ cup mixed diced organic red, yellow, and green bell peppers (2 tablespoons plus 2 teaspoons of each type)

½ cup diced red onions

1 cup heavy cream

½ teaspoon minced jalapeño chile or red pepper flakes

2 teaspoons chopped fresh chives

2 teaspoons chopped fresh dill

2 teaspoons chopped fresh flat-leaf parsley

Leaves from 2 fresh thyme sprigs, chopped

½ teaspoon salt

⅛ teaspoon cayenne pepper

1 extra-large cage-free egg, lightly beaten

1 cup *panko* (Japanese bread crumbs)

1 cup ground almonds

1¼ pounds fresh lump crabmeat, picked over for cartilage and shell fragments

5 tablespoons unsalted butter, at room temperature

2 tablespoons vegetable oil, plus more as needed

6 English muffins, split

12 extra-large cage-free eggs

Salt

Chopped fresh chives for garnish

**For the crab cakes:** Make the crab mixture and shape the cakes at least 1 hour before you are ready to cook them. In a 10-inch skillet, heat the olive oil over medium-high heat. Add the bell peppers and onions and sauté, stirring frequently, until tender, 7 to 9 minutes. Using a slotted spoon, transfer to a bowl and let cool.

While the pepper mixture is cooling, return the skillet to medium-high heat, add the cream and jalapeño chile, and simmer briskly, stirring frequently, until the cream is reduced by half, about 5 minutes. Add to the pepper mixture and let cool for about 15 minutes.

Add the chives, dill, parsley, thyme, salt, and cayenne to the cooled mixture and stir well. Stir in the egg and half each of the bread crumbs and almonds. Gently fold in the crabmeat; the mixture should be lumpy.

On a plate, stir together the remaining bread crumbs and almonds. Have ready a baking sheet. With clean hands, divide the crab mixture into 12 equal portions (each will weigh about 2½ ounces), then shape each portion into a cake the diameter of an English muffin. As you form each cake, gently press both sides of it into the crumb-almond mixture to coat well, then place on the baking sheet. When all of the cakes are ready, cover the pan loosely with plastic wrap and refrigerate for at least 1 hour or up to 3 hours.

**To cook and serve the crab cakes:** Preheat the oven to 200°F. Have ready a large baking dish. In a large skillet, combine 2 tablespoons of the butter

and the 2 tablespoons vegetable oil over medium-high heat. When the butter is melted, add half of the crab cakes and sauté, carefully turning them once with a spatula, until they are golden brown on both sides and cooked through, about 4 minutes on each side. Transfer to the baking dish and keep warm in the oven while you cook the remaining crab cakes the same way, adding more oil to the pan if needed to prevent sticking.

When the crab cakes are almost done cooking, toast the English muffins and spread them lightly with a little of the remaining butter. Place 1 or 2 muffin halves, cut side up, on each individual serving plate, or place them all on 1 or 2 large platters.

**To cook the eggs and serve:** As soon as all of the crab cakes are cooked and in the oven, wipe out the skillet, return it to medium-high heat, and melt enough of the remaining butter in it to coat the bottom evenly when you swirl the pan. Carefully crack just enough eggs into the pan to fit without crowding and sprinkle them with salt. Fry until the whites are set and the yolks are cooked to your or your guest's liking, spooning a little of the butter from the pan over the whites and yolks to help them set, 3 to 5 minutes. Transfer the same number of crab cakes to muffin halves as eggs you cooked, and top each crab cake with a fried egg. Repeat with the remaining butter, eggs, and crab cakes. Garnish the eggs with the chives and serve right away.

"Bread pudding is great for entertaining because you can serve it hot, warm, or at room temperature. Frozen spring and summer fruits bring bright, festive color and flavor to this winter dessert."

# White Chocolate Berry–Cherry Bread Pudding

**SERVES 8**

5 cups cubed stale brioche, challah, croissants, or crustless French bread (1-inch cubes)

Butter-flavored or plain nonstick cooking spray

3 cups whole milk

1 cup heavy cream

1 cup sugar

1 teaspoon pure vanilla extract

4 large cage-free eggs

4 large cage-free egg yolks

Pinch of salt

¾ cup white chocolate chips

1½ cups frozen mixed berries and/or frozen pitted cherries

Preheat the oven to 350°F.

Spread the bread cubes on a rimmed baking sheet, place in the oven, and toast until golden brown, 8 to 10 minutes. Remove the bread cubes from the oven, but leave the oven on.

Generously spray a 12-inch round ovenproof pan or a 3-quart baking dish with nonstick spray. Transfer the bread cubes to the pan, spreading them evenly.

In a large saucepan, combine the milk, cream, and sugar over medium heat and bring to a simmer, stirring to dissolve the sugar. Stir in the vanilla and remove from the heat.

In a medium bowl, whisk together the eggs, egg yolks, and salt. Slowly pour ½ cup of the hot milk mixture into the eggs while whisking continuously. Then, while whisking the milk mixture in the pan continuously, carefully pour the egg mixture into the pan, using a rubber spatula to scrape every bit from the bowl.

Pour the custard mixture evenly over the bread cubes and let stand at room temperature for 5 minutes. Then, using the spatula or the back of a large spoon, gently press the bread down into the custard mixture. Sprinkle the white chocolate chips evenly over the top, and fold them gently into the bread mixture. Evenly spread the berries and/or cherries on top.

Place the baking dish inside a larger roasting pan. Open the oven door, pull out the center rack most of the way, but not so far that it will tip when the pan is set on it. Set the roasting pan holding the baking dish on the rack, and then pour hot water into the roasting pan to reach about halfway up the sides of the baking dish. Slowly slide the rack into the oven and close the oven door. Bake until the pudding appears just set in the center when the baking dish is gently jiggled and the top is just beginning to color, about 45 minutes.

Remove the roasting pan from the oven, being careful to avoid splashing the water, and lift the baking dish out of the pan. Serve the pudding hot, warm, or at room temperature.

# Holiday Nut and Coconut Brittle

**MAKES ABOUT 1¾ POUNDS**

½ cup shredded unsweetened coconut

2 cups unsalted mixed nuts

1¼ cups sugar

⅓ cup light corn syrup

⅓ cup water

1 cup unsalted butter, cut into small pieces

Vegetable oil or nonstick cooking spray

1 teaspoon salt

½ teaspoon baking soda

Preheat the oven to 350°F. Spread the coconut on a rimmed baking sheet, place in the oven, and toast, stirring once after about 3 minutes to ensure even toasting, until just pale gold, 6 to 8 minutes. Pour onto a plate and let cool. Leave the oven on.

Spread the nuts on the same baking sheet, place in the oven, and toast, stirring the nuts once after 5 minutes to ensure even toasting, until lightly golden, 8 to 10 minutes. Remove from the oven and let cool. Transfer the cooled nuts to a food processor and pulse a few times to chop coarsely, then set aside.

In a deep, heavy saucepan, stir together the sugar, corn syrup, and water and bring to a boil over medium heat. Boil, without stirring, until a layer of bubbles forms on top, 3 to 4 minutes. Cover the pan with aluminum foil and continue to boil, undisturbed, for 5 minutes longer.

Remove the foil, add the butter, and stir with a wooden spoon until the butter has melted and is fully combined with the sugar mixture. Continue cooking over medium heat, stirring occasionally, until a candy thermometer inserted into the mixture registers 300°F, about 30 minutes. Meanwhile, coat a 12-by-17-inch rimmed baking sheet with vegetable oil.

As soon as the sugar mixture reaches the desired temperature, remove from the heat and immediately but carefully stir in the salt, baking soda, coconut, and nuts. Pour the mixture into the prepared pan and, working quickly, use a long metal spatula to spread it as thinly and evenly as possible over the entire bottom of the pan. Let the brittle cool to room temperature and harden, 20 to 30 minutes.

Run a clean, dry kitchen towel over the surface to absorb some of the oil. Neatly cut the brittle with a chef's knife, or tap it with a mallet to break it into irregular pieces. Store the brittle in 1 or more airtight containers at cool room temperature until you are ready to pack it in individual plastic bags. It will keep for up to 1 week.

"Especially during the holidays, I like to send my guests home with a little gift of food to enjoy later. Pack pieces of this crunchy toffee brittle into small plastic bags and tie them with colorful ribbons for an easy holiday treat."

# TIM SCOTT

# HOLIDAY OPEN HOUSE

A casual open house with a spread of special-occasion food is a great solution for the holidays. You can do most of the work in advance, so once the guests arrive, all you have to do is restock the buffet. Tim's fresh, colorful menu is a perfect mix of light nibbles and heartier fare. It's ideal for a drop-in party, and easy to scale up for a bigger gathering.

# Candied Walnuts

"These are the best candied walnuts ever. They make a great snack or gift, and I like to use them on salads and ice cream sundaes, too. Be sure to spray both the parchment in the pan and the parchment you pour the hot nuts onto with nonstick spray. The nuts are very sticky until they cool down."

**MAKES ABOUT 6 CUPS**

Nonstick cooking spray

½ cup honey

⅓ cup firmly packed light brown sugar

2 pounds walnut halves

Preheat the oven to 350°F.

Line 2 rimmed baking sheets with parchment paper, and spray the parchment with nonstick spray. Spray 2 additional baking sheet–sized pieces of parchment with nonstick spray and place them on a work surface.

In a large bowl, stir together the honey and brown sugar. Set aside.

Set a steamer basket or steamer insert in a large saucepan or a stockpot. Add water to the pan, filling to just below the bottom of the basket. Place the walnuts in the basket, cover the pan with a tight-filling lid, and place over high heat. Bring to a boil and steam until the walnuts are thoroughly heated and moistened by the steam, 2 to 3 minutes.

Carefully remove the steamer basket from the pan and dump the nuts into the bowl with the sugar-honey mixture. Using a heat-resistant rubber spatula, toss well to coat the nuts evenly. Spread the nuts evenly on the 2 prepared pans. Bake, stirring once after 7 to 8 minutes, until the nuts are well caramelized, 15 to 20 minutes.

When the nuts are ready, remove the pans from the oven and carefully pour each pan of nuts onto a prepared sheet of parchment. Spread the nuts with the rubber spatula into a single, even layer. Let cool to room temperature, breaking up any clumps, then transfer to a bowl to serve. The nuts may be stored in an airtight container at room temperature for up to 7 days.

# Spicy Peanuts

"I came up with this recipe years ago for a TV segment on unusual game-day snacks, and I've been making them ever since. They're simple to prepare and addictively sweet and spicy."

**MAKES 2¼ CUPS**

2¼ cups unsalted peanuts

1 tablespoon sugar

1 tablespoon *sambal oelek* (Southeast Asian chile paste)

1 teaspoon kosher salt

1 teaspoon freshly ground black pepper

Preheat the oven to 350°F.

Spread the peanuts on a rimmed baking sheet and toast in the oven, stirring once, until they take on color and are fragrant, 6 to 7 minutes.

While the peanuts are in the oven, in a medium bowl, stir together the sugar, *sambal oelek*, salt, and pepper.

When the peanuts are ready, immediately add them to the seasonings in the medium bowl and toss to coat the peanuts evenly. Serve immediately, or let cool, transfer to an airtight container, and store at room temperature for up to 1 week.

# Tricolor Deviled Quail Eggs

**MAKES 36 STUFFED EGGS**

18 quail eggs

⅓ cup mayonnaise

⅛ teaspoon kosher salt

⅛ teaspoon freshly ground black pepper

½ teaspoon wasabi paste

½ teaspoon beet juice

2 tablespoons finely diced cold-smoked salmon

½ teaspoon chopped fresh dill, plus more for garnish

Chopped fresh chives for garnish

Matchstick-cut, peeled Chioggia beet for garnish

Crushed wasabi peas for garnish

Caviar for garnish

In a small saucepan, combine the quail eggs with water to cover over medium-high heat and bring to a boil. Meanwhile, prepare an ice bath. When the water reaches a boil, reduce the heat and cook the eggs at a gentle simmer for 5 minutes. Immediately remove from the heat, drain, and immerse in the ice water bath to cool completely.

Peel the cooled eggs, cut in half lengthwise, and remove the yolks, being careful not to tear the whites. As you slice each egg, set the halved whites on your work surface and put the yolks in a medium bowl. Using a fork, mash the yolks and then stir in the mayonnaise, salt, and pepper.

Divide the yolk mixture evenly among 3 small bowls. Stir the wasabi paste into the first bowl, the beet juice into the second bowl, and the smoked salmon and dill into the third bowl. Using a small rubber spatula or spoon, transfer the wasabi–egg yolk mixture

to a small pastry bag fitted with a ¼-inch round tip (or a snack-sized zippered plastic bag with a tiny bit of a bottom corner snipped off). Pipe the wasabi–egg yolk mixture into 12 of the egg white halves. Repeat with the beet–egg yolk mixture, filling 12 egg white halves, and then with the salmon–egg yolk mixture, filling the remaining 12 egg white halves.

Arrange the filled eggs attractively on a platter. Garnish the wasabi-flavored eggs with a sprinkle of the wasabi peas, the beet-flavored eggs with the chives and Chioggia beets, and the salmon-flavored eggs with a tiny dollop of caviar and a bit of dill. Serve immediately.

**TIM'S TIP:** It's a good idea to boil a few extra quail eggs in case any fall apart when you peel them. You can also use chicken eggs to make this recipe. For 12 eggs, multiply the other ingredients by 4 to make 24 stuffed halves.

"I think of these as deviled-egg shooters, because they're so small and intense. The fun is in the garnishes, which add a lot of color, flavor, and eye appeal."

TIM SCOTT

# Roasted Beet Salad

"I've won over a lot of beet skeptics with this salad. The roasted beets are like candy, and the citrus, peppery arugula, and creamy goat cheese go perfectly with that sweetness. The candy-cane Chioggia beet sticks really add to the holiday effect.

**SERVES 12 TO 16**

4 or 5 medium golden beets

4 or 5 medium red beets

4 or 5 medium Chioggia beets, plus 1 beet for garnish

3 tablespoons olive oil

Salt and freshly ground black pepper

4 or 5 clementines, oranges, or blood oranges

¼ cup extra virgin olive oil, plus more for serving (optional)

5 ounces baby arugula

1 cup crumbled Yarra Valley feta cheese or other good-quality feta or fresh goat cheese

8 small fresh basil sprigs, top leaves only

¼ bunch fresh chives, finely sliced

Preheat the oven to 400°F.

If the beets have the tops attached, trim off the tops, leaving 1 inch of the stem intact, and reserve the tops for another use or discard. Lay 3 large pieces of aluminum foil on a work surface. Place the golden beets in the center of 1 piece of foil. Drizzle them with 1 tablespoon of the olive oil, season generously with salt and pepper, and then roll the beets around a bit to coat them with the oil and seasoning. Crimp the edges of the foil together tightly to form a sealed packet. Repeat with the red beets and the Chioggia beets in separate packets, using 1 tablespoon of the oil for each packet; reserve 1 raw Chioggia beet for garnish.

Place the packets on a rimmed baking sheet and roast the beets in the oven until they can be easily pierced with a fork (open the top of a packet to test), 30 to 45 minutes. Remove from the oven and let the beets cool until they can be handled. Then, using your hands or a paper towel, rub off the skins. Trim off the stem ends and cut each beet into 6 or 8 bite-sized wedges. Set aside.

Cut a thin slice off the top and bottom of each clementine to reveal the flesh. Stand 1 clementine upright on a cutting board. Using a sharp knife and following the contour of the fruit, cut downward to remove the peel and pith. Repeat with the remaining clementines. Holding a peeled clementine over a bowl, cut along both sides of each segment to free it from the membrane, catching the segments and any juice in the bowl. Repeat with the remaining clementines.

Retrieve 2 tablespoons of the clementine juice from the bowl and add to a large bowl. Whisk the olive oil into the clementine juice, then season with salt and pepper. Add the beets and toss gently to coat with the dressing. Taste and adjust the seasoning with salt and pepper.

Arrange the arugula in a bed on a large platter. Top with the beet wedges, scattered randomly. Using a slotted spoon, transfer the citrus wedges to the platter, scattering them over the beets. Top with the cheese. Drizzle the salad with a little more olive oil, if desired, and some citrus juice. Sprinkle with the basil and chives. Peel the raw Chioggia beet, cut into julienne, and sprinkle over the salad. Serve right away.

# Mushroom-Crusted Strip Roast

**SERVES 16**

1 whole New York strip loin, about 12 pounds

2 ounces mixed dried mushrooms

4 tablespoons olive oil

¼ cup fresh thyme leaves

2 tablespoons kosher salt

2 tablespoons freshly ground black pepper

Tomato Chile Jam (recipe follows)

Garlic-Scented Mushrooms (recipe follows)

Preheat the oven to 375°F. Line a rimmed baking sheet with aluminum foil, and place a rack in the pan large enough to hold the beef (or use 2 racks).

Trim off the silver skin and any visible fat from the strip loin. Cut the loin in half crosswise, and then cut each half in half lengthwise. You will end up with 4 pieces, each weighing about 2 pounds.

Working in batches if necessary, grind the dried mushrooms in a blender or spice grinder to a fine powder, about 1 minute. Transfer the mushroom powder to a large plate. Rub the beef pieces on all sides with 2 tablespoons of the olive oil, and season on all sides with the thyme, salt, and pepper. Roll each piece of seasoned beef in the mushroom powder, coating evenly.

In a heavy-bottomed sauté pan, heat 1 tablespoon of the olive oil over medium-high heat. Add 2 pieces of the beef and sear, turning them once, until browned on both sides, 2 to 3 minutes on each side. Transfer the seared beef to the rack in the prepared baking sheet. Repeat with the remaining 2 pieces of beef and the remaining 1 tablespoon oil.

Roast the beef until an instant-read thermometer inserted into the thickest part of a loin piece registers 120° to 125°F for medium-rare. If the pieces are not all the same size, check each one individually, as some may cook faster than others.

Remove from the oven, tent with aluminum foil, and let rest for 10 minutes. Using a sharp knife, cut against the grain into slices and arrange on a platter. Serve with the jam and mushrooms on the side.

## Tomato Chile Jam

Serve this chutney-style condiment with the strip loin. If you have extra, it keeps forever in the fridge, and it's really good on any kind of roasted meat and grilled seafood.

MAKES ABOUT 3 CUPS

2⅓ cups (20 ounces) good-quality canned diced tomatoes (preferably Pomi brand)

1 red jalapeño chile, coarsely chopped

4 cloves garlic, coarsely chopped

2 tablespoons chopped, peeled ginger

2 tablespoons Asian fish sauce

1¾ cups firmly packed light brown sugar

½ cup sherry vinegar

In a blender, combine half of the tomatoes with the chile, garlic, ginger, and fish sauce and process until a smooth purée forms.

Pour the purée into a deep, heavy-bottomed saucepan and place over medium heat. Add the brown sugar and vinegar and stir constantly until the mixture comes to a boil. Stir in the remaining tomatoes, reduce the heat to medium-low, and simmer gently, stirring occasionally and scraping any solids from the bottom and sides of the pan, until the mixture has a thick, jam-like consistency, 30 to 40 minutes.

Remove from the heat and let cool to room temperature before serving. Or, transfer the cooled jam to an airtight container and refrigerate for up to 1 week, then bring to room temperature before serving.

## Garlic-Scented Mushrooms

You can make this dish with any kind of mushrooms. The key is to get a good sear on them. That means letting them sit still in the hot pan and not overstirring. To keep the garlic from burning, I start it on top of the mushrooms for the first few minutes, then stir it in.

MAKES ABOUT 3¾ CUPS

½ cup plus 1 tablespoon butter

6 ounces shiitake mushrooms, stemmed and sliced

6 ounces oyster mushrooms, sliced

12 ounces button mushrooms, as small as possible, left whole if small or halved or quartered if large

3 teaspoons minced garlic

3 teaspoons fresh thyme leaves

1½ teaspoons kosher salt

1½ teaspoons freshly ground pepper

3 teaspoons porcini or truffle oil (optional)

3 teaspoons chopped fresh flat-leaf parsley

In a large, heavy-bottomed sauté pan, melt 2 tablespoons of the butter over high heat. Add one-third of each type of mushroom, 1 teaspoon of the garlic, 1 teaspoon of the thyme, ½ teaspoon of the salt, and ½ teaspoon of the pepper all at once and sear, without tossing or stirring, for 3 minutes. When the mushrooms are seared on one side, gently toss them once to turn them, then let them sear without disturbing on the second side for 1 or 2 minutes. When the mushrooms are well seared on both sides, remove the pan from the heat and add 1 tablespoon of the butter, 1 teaspoon of the porcini oil (if using), and 1 teaspoon of the parsley and toss to combine. Transfer the mushrooms to a serving platter, and clean the pan thoroughly. Repeat the process two more times with the remaining mushrooms and other ingredients, adding each batch to the platter.

Serve the mushrooms warm. Or, let cool to room temperature, cover, and refrigerate for up to 24 hours, then bring to room temperature before serving.

"You see a lot of roasted beef tenderloins on buffets. I prefer the strip loin, which has much more flavor. This is great at room temperature as a buffet main course, and you can serve rolls on the side for making sandwiches."

"A trifle is an easy way to serve an elegant dessert to a lot of people. If you've got a little more time, make individual servings by layering the same ingredients in martini glasses."

# Lemon Raspberry Trifle

**SERVES 16 TO 20**

## LEMON CURD

12 egg yolks

3 cups sugar

1 cup fresh lemon juice

1½ cups unsalted butter, at room temperature, cut into small cubes

3 tablespoons grated lemon zest

## LEMON SYRUP

½ cup granulated sugar

5 tablespoons fresh lemon juice

¼ cup water

2 pounds raspberries

¾ cup sugar

1 (1-pound) good-quality pound cake, cut into 1-inch cubes (about 10 cups)

Whipped cream for serving

Fresh mint sprigs for garnish

**For the lemon curd:** Pour water to a depth of about 3 inches into a medium-sized saucepan and bring to a gentle simmer over medium heat. Meanwhile, in a metal bowl that will rest in the rim of the saucepan, whisk together the egg yolks, sugar, and lemon juice until blended. Set the bowl over (not touching) the simmering water and stir the mixture until it is warm, 3 to 4 minutes. Add the butter and lemon zest and continue to stir until the mixture thickens to a puddinglike consistency and registers 170°F on an instant-read thermometer, 10 to 15 minutes. Remove the bowl from the pan and pour the curd into a clean medium bowl. Cover the bowl with plastic wrap, pressing it directly onto the surface of the curd to prevent a skin from forming. You should have about 6 cups curd. Refrigerate until well chilled, at least 4 hours or up to 4 days.

**For the lemon syrup:** In a small saucepan, combine the sugar, lemon juice, and water and bring to a boil over medium heat, stirring to dissolve the sugar. Remove from the heat and let cool to room temperature. Use immediately, or cover and refrigerate for up to 3 days.

In a large bowl, combine the raspberries and sugar and mash gently with a fork until most of the raspberries are bruised and their juices are beginning to flow. Cover and refrigerate for at least 30 minutes or up to 3 days.

Arrange half of the cake cubes snugly in the bottom of a 4-quart footed trifle dish or glass bowl. Drizzle the cake with half of the lemon syrup. Spoon half of the lemon curd on top and, using a small offset spatula, spread it gently and evenly over the cake cubes. Pour half of the raspberries evenly over the lemon curd. Top with the remaining cake cubes, followed by the remaining lemon syrup, the remaining lemon curd, and finally the remaining raspberries. Cover with plastic wrap and refrigerate for at least 1 hour or up to overnight.

Just before serving, garnish the trifle with the whipped cream and mint sprigs.

# RICK BAYLESS

# CHRISTMAS AT HOME

When Rick and his family sit down to a cozy Christmas dinner at home, what they're hungry for are soulful, comforting dishes that riff on their favorite Mexican flavors and traditions. You can make everything on this menu ahead of time, so when your guests arrive, all you have to do is carve up the turkey and you're good to go.

"The bright crimson of this famous Mexican Christmas punch always puts people in a holiday mood. *Tejocote*—the sweet-tart fruit of the hawthorn, reminiscent of a crab apple—comes into season at Christmastime, and it's the defining ingredient of this drink."

# Warm Christmas Punch

*Ponche Navideño*

**MAKES 2½ QUARTS; SERVES ABOUT 10**

1½ quarts plus 3 cups water

About 9 ounces (1¾ cups roughly chopped) *piloncillo* (Mexican unrefined cone sugar), or 1½ cups firmly packed dark brown sugar

2 cups (about 2 ounces) dried *jamaica* flowers (dried hibiscus flowers)

⅓ cup (about 1½ ounces) raisins

⅓ cup (about 1½ ounces) chopped prunes

1 large apple, peeled, cored, and diced (about 2 cups)

3 pieces fresh sugarcane, each 2 inches long, peeled and cut lengthwise into ¼-inch slivers

1½ cups jarred guavas or *tejocotes* (or some of each), drained

1 cup rum (optional)

In a large saucepan, bring the 1½ quarts water to a boil. Add the *piloncillo* and stir until dissolved. Add the *jamaica* flowers and let the water return to a boil, then remove from the heat, cover, and let steep for 30 minutes. Strain the liquid through a fine-mesh sieve and return it to the saucepan.

Add the remaining 3 cups water, the raisins, prunes, apple, and sugarcane to the pan and set over medium-low heat. If using guavas, cut each one in half, scrape out the seeds, cut the flesh into ½-inch strips, and add to the pot; if using *tejocotes*, add them whole. Bring the *ponche* to a simmer and simmer gently for 15 to 20 minutes.

Just before serving, add the rum, if using, then ladle the *ponche* into mugs, adding a mixture of fruit and sugarcane for each guest. A spoon is not an inappropriate addition to each mug.

"If there's a Latin grocery near you, look for fresh calabaza, the tan or green Mexican pumpkin with bright orange flesh, usually sold in big chunks. I like to set off its sweet flavor with a little apple and a bit of smoky chipotle."

# Roasted Butternut Squash Soup
## with Apples and Chipotle

**SERVES 8**

### SOUP

2 tablespoons olive oil

1 teaspoon ground cinnamon
(preferably Mexican)

Salt

2½ pounds Mexican pumpkin (calabaza),
split into wedges, seeds discarded,
or 1 medium (about 2½ pounds)
butternut squash, split in half
lengthwise, seeds discarded

1 medium (about 6 ounces) white
onion, diced

1 firm cooking apple such as Granny
Smith, peeled, quartered, and cored

2 to 3 canned *chipotle chiles en adobo*,
seeds discarded, roughly chopped

5 cups chicken broth

About 1 tablespoon sugar, if using
Mexican pumpkin (calabaza)

### CROUTONS

3 tablespoons unsalted butter, cubed

¼ teaspoon chipotle chile powder

½ teaspoon ground cinnamon
(preferably Mexican)

1½ teaspoons sugar

¼ teaspoon salt

3 cups (about 5 ounces) cubed
firm-textured, day-old, crust-free
bread (½-inch cubes)

Preheat the oven to 425°F degrees.
Line 3 rimmed baking sheets with
aluminum foil.

**For the soup:** In a large bowl, stir
together the olive oil, ½ teaspoon of
the cinnamon, and a scant ½ teaspoon
salt. Brush part of the mixture over the
cut edges of the pumpkin (or squash).
Place the pumpkin (or squash) cut side
down on a prepared baking sheet.
Scoop the onion and apple into the
bowl and toss to coat with the remaining olive oil mixture. Spread onto a
separate prepared baking sheet. Slide
both baking sheets into the oven and
roast until the pumpkin (or squash) is
soft and the onion-apple mixture is
golden brown, about 1 hour for the
Mexican pumpkin (or 40 to 50 minutes
for the squash) and 40 to 50 minutes
for the onion-apple mixture. Halfway
through the cooking time, stir the
onion-apple mixture. Remove both
baking sheets from the oven and
reduce the oven temperature to 350°F.

Scoop the onion mixture into a
large (4-quart) soup pot. Using a large
spoon, scrape the pumpkin (or squash)
flesh from its skin into the pot, then
add the chipotle chiles, ½ teaspoon salt,
and the remaining ½ teaspoon cinnamon. Stir in the broth, bring to a simmer
over medium heat, and simmer for
30 minutes.

**For the croutons:** While the soup is
simmering, in a large, microwave-safe
bowl, combine the butter, chipotle
chile powder, cinnamon, sugar, and
salt. Microwave on full power for
1 minute until the butter melts, then
stir. Scoop the cubed bread into the
butter mixture and toss to coat. Spread
the coated bread cubes on the third
prepared baking sheet and bake until
the croutons are golden brown and
crisp, 10 to 12 minutes.

**To serve:** Working in batches if necessary, transfer the soup to a blender and
process to a smooth purée. Return the
soup to the pot and bring back to a
simmer. Taste and season with salt,
usually ½ teaspoon. If using Mexican
pumpkin, you'll also need to add about
1 tablespoon sugar. Ladle into warmed
soup bowls and sprinkle the seasoned
croutons on top.

# Mesquite-Smoked Grilled Turkey
## with Red Chile Adobo Sauce

**SERVES 8**

1 fresh whole turkey, 12 to 14 pounds

2 gallons plus 1 cup water

1 cup firmly packed dark brown sugar

1 cup salt

1 tablespoon red pepper flakes

6 cloves garlic, crushed

1 bunch fresh marjoram sprigs or
   1 tablespoon dried leaf marjoram

1 bunch fresh thyme sprigs or
   1 tablespoon dried leaf thyme

10 to 12 bay leaves

1 tablespoon olive oil

Red Chile Adobo Sauce (page 122)

Jícama-Cranberry Relish (page 122)

Note: You will need 2 cups of mesquite
   chips for smoking.

**To brine the turkey:** If the turkey has a metal clamp on its legs, remove it. Remove the giblets and neck from the cavity and reserve for another use. (They can be used for making the broth for the Red Chile Adobo Sauce that follows.) Rinse the bird well and pat dry with paper towels. Place 2 large food-safe plastic bags (we like Reynolds turkey-sized oven bags), one inside the other, in a large, clean, deep dishpan or plastic bucket. Add 1 gallon of the water, the sugar, salt, and pepper flakes, and stir to dissolve the sugar and salt. Add the remaining 1 gallon water and stir to mix. Place the turkey, breast side down, in the mixture, making sure it is completely immersed in the brine.

Squeeze the air out of the bags and tie them securely closed. Refrigerate for at least 12 hours or up to overnight.

To set up the grill for indirect cooking: Soak 2 cups mesquite chips in water to cover for at least 30 minutes. Preheat a gas grill to medium-high, or light a fire in a charcoal grill and let it burn just until the coals are covered with gray ash and very hot.

When the grill is ready, turn the burner(s) in the center of the gas grill to medium-low, or bank the coals to the sides of the charcoal grill. Add some of the soaked wood chips to the grill (for a gas grill, place them in a smoker box or wrap the chips in foil and poke holes in the foil; for charcoal, place them on the hot coals). For the charcoal grill, set the grill grate in place.

**To prepare the turkey for the grill:** Remove the turkey from the brine, and discard the brine. Pat the turkey thoroughly dry with paper towels. (If you are not cooking the turkey at this point, place it in the outer roasting bag, which should be dry and clean, and store it in the refrigerator.) Rub the turkey cavity with the crushed garlic. Stuff the herbs and bay leaves in the cavity, then tie the legs together with cotton string. Pull the skin over the neck opening and secure with a small skewer. Set the

turkey on a roasting rack set inside a heavy-gauge aluminum foil pan. Brush the turkey lightly with the olive oil.

**To grill the turkey:** Set the turkey in the pan on the grill grate away from the fire. Pour the remaining 1 cup water into the pan, and cover the grill. To maintain an even temperature with a charcoal grill, add more coals regularly (usually a few pieces every 30 minutes or so). Keep adding wood chips as desired to give smokiness.

Check the turkey periodically. You may want to cover the wing tips and/or the whole turkey to prevent the skin from getting too brown. The turkey is done if when a thigh joint is pierced, the juices run clear, or when an instant-read thermometer inserted into the thickest part of a thigh registers about 155°F. Estimate 12 to 14 minutes per pound, or typically 2½ to 3 hours for a 12- to 14-pound turkey. When the turkey is ready, remove it from the grill, cover loosely with foil, and let stand for 15 minutes. (The temperature will rise 5 to 10 degrees while the turkey is resting.)

Carve the turkey and arrange on a warmed platter. Serve with the warm Red Chile Adobo Sauce and the Jícama-Cranberry Relish.

"For Christmas or Thanksgiving, a smoked turkey is a great way to go, satisfying the cravings of poultry and smoked ham lovers alike. All you need is a grill and some mesquite chips."

# Red Chile Adobo Sauce

"This wonderfully earthy sauce suggests all kinds of possibilities for enjoying the turkey leftovers the next day—in sandwiches, tucked into warm tortillas, or over greens."

**MAKES ABOUT 5 CUPS**

**ADOBO PURÉE**

⅓ cup vegetable oil

12 medium (about 6 ounces) dried ancho chiles, stemmed, seeded, and torn into flat pieces

4 cups hot water

6 cloves garlic, roughly chopped

2 teaspoons dried oregano (preferably Mexican)

1 teaspoon freshly ground black pepper

½ teaspoon ground cumin (preferably freshly ground)

¼ teaspoon ground cloves (preferably freshly ground)

½ cup cider vinegar

4 cups chicken or turkey broth (if desired, use the turkey neck and giblets from the grilled turkey for making the broth)

Salt

2 to 3 tablespoons sugar

**For the adobo purée:** In a large skillet, heat the vegetable oil over medium heat until it shimmers. Add the chiles, 1 or 2 pieces at a time, and oil-toast them, turning them once, until they smell very toasty and are blistered, only a few seconds per side. As they are ready, transfer them to a large bowl. When all of the chile pieces are toasted, pour off all but a generous film of oil from the skillet and set the skillet aside.

Add the hot water to the chiles, place a small plate on top to keep the chiles submerged, and let rehydrate for about 20 minutes.

Measure the garlic, oregano, pepper, cumin, cloves, and vinegar into a blender or food processor. Pour in the rehydrated chiles, liquid and all (do this in two batches if necessary). Process the mixture to a smooth purée. Press through a medium-mesh sieve set over a bowl.

**To finish the sauce:** Set the chile-frying skillet over medium heat. When it is quite hot, add the adobo purée and cook, stirring, until the purée is reduced to the thickness of tomato paste, about 10 minutes. Stir in the broth, reduce the heat to medium-low, and simmer for 30 minutes or so. The finished sauce should have a light texture—not watery, but just one stage thicker. (A good test is to pour a little on a plate and watch it spread: If it flows evenly, it's just right. If it doesn't flow much and water begins separating around the edges, it's too thick.) Season with salt (usually about 1 tablespoon) and with the sugar to taste. It should taste a little sweet and sour with a hint of saltiness. Serve warm.

**Working ahead:** The finished sauce will keep in a tightly covered container in the refrigerator for a few days.

# Jícama-Cranberry Relish

**MAKES ABOUT 3½ CUPS**

1 large red onion, finely diced (about 1½ cups)

1½ cups finely diced, peeled jícama

½ cup chopped dried cranberries

3 tablespoons cider vinegar

Salt

6 tablespoons coarsely chopped fresh cilantro

In a bowl, combine the onion, jícama, dried cranberries, and vinegar and stir to mix. Taste and season with a little salt. Stir in the cilantro.

The relish is best when served within 2 hours.

"This refreshing relish made with crunchy jícama and chewy dried cranberries would make a great alternative to traditional cranberry sauce on any Thanksgiving menu."

"Flan is the perfect soothing finish to a meal of bold, spicy flavors. If you can't find passion fruit, go with a sprinkling of diced kiwifruit or toasted unsweetened coconut."

# Coconut Flan

*Flan de Coco*

## CARAMEL

1 cup sugar

2 tablespoons light corn syrup

⅛ teaspoon fresh lemon juice

2 tablespoons water

## CUSTARD

¾ cup sugar

1 cup whole milk

1 (13½-ounce) can coconut milk

3 large eggs

5 large egg yolks

1½ teaspoons pure vanilla extract (preferably Mexican)

2 or 3 passion fruits for garnish

**For the caramel:** Set eight ¾-cup molds (custard cups, coffee cups, or individual soufflé dishes) in a roasting pan that's at least 2 inches deep and large enough to space the molds at least ½ inch apart. In a microwave-safe container (a 1-quart glass measuring pitcher works well), stir together the sugar, corn syrup, lemon juice, and water. Microwave on full power until the mixture is light brown, 4 to 5 minutes (the timing will depend on the power of your microwave). Remove from the microwave and let the sugar syrup sit for 4 minutes to finish cooking and to darken to a deep caramel color.

Immediately pour the caramel into the molds, dividing it evenly and tilting each mold so the caramel completely covers the bottom. Leave the molds in the roasting pan.

**To make the custard:** Preheat the oven to 325°F. Bring a tea kettle filled with water to a simmer. In a medium (3-quart) saucepan, combine the sugar, whole milk, and coconut milk, set over medium heat, and bring to a simmer. Meanwhile, in a large bowl, whisk together the eggs and egg yolks until thoroughly blended. When the milk mixture is at a simmer, remove from the heat and slowly add to the eggs while whisking constantly. Stir in the vanilla and strain through a fine-mesh sieve into a pitcher or bowl. Pour or ladle the custard into the molds, dividing it evenly.

**To bake the flans:** Open the oven door and pull out the center oven rack most of the way, but not so far that it will tip when the pan is set on it. Set the pan holding the molds on the rack, then slowly pour the simmering water into the pan to reach two-thirds of the way up the sides of the molds. Slowly slide the rack into the oven, and close the oven door. Bake until the flans are set in the middle, 50 to 60 minutes. Remove from the oven and let cool in the water bath, about 1 hour. Then remove from the water bath and refrigerate the flans until thoroughly chilled, about 2 hours.

**To unmold and serve the flans:** Run a small knife around the inside edge of a mold to release the flan from the sides of the mold. Invert a small serving plate over the mold, grasp the plate and mold firmly, and reverse the two together. Shake the flan up and down, back and forth until you hear it drop onto the plate. Lift off the mold and scrape any remaining caramel out of the mold and onto the flan. Repeat with the remaining flans.

Cut open the passion fruits and scoop out the seeds and juice. Spoon them around each flan. Dessert's ready.

## TODD ENGLISH

# FEAST OF THE SEVEN FISHES

It's a southern Italian tradition to gather with family and friends on Christmas Eve for a seven-course seafood dinner. When Todd was growing up, Christmas Eve always meant seafood, though it was never seven courses. For this menu, he's come up with a tasty compromise: four savory courses featuring a total of seven kinds of seafood.

# Tuna Crudo

"Go for quality here. The best sushi-grade tuna you can get your hands on and some good sea salt will make all the difference. Whenever I have an ingredient from the sea, I season it with sea salt to put a little oceany flavor back into the dish."

**SERVES 6**

1 English cucumber, cut into ¼-inch dice

¼ cup sherry vinegar

¼ cup extra virgin olive oil

3 fresh flat-leaf parsley sprigs, chopped

3 fresh cilantro sprigs, chopped

Sea salt and freshly ground black pepper

1 pound sushi-grade tuna fillet

Put the cucumber in a bowl. Add the vinegar and then drizzle in the olive oil while stirring constantly, coating the cucumber evenly. Add the parsley and cilantro and season with salt and pepper. Set aside.

Using your sharpest knife, cut the tuna against the grain into thin slices (about ⅛ inch thick). Divide the tuna slices evenly among individual serving plates, shingling them attractively. Spoon the cucumber vinaigrette over the tuna and serve immediately.

"Instead of the usual boiled shrimp or crab cocktail, I like to marinate and grill the seafood. The crab claws will be cooked when you buy them, so you're not really cooking them on the grill. You're just infusing them with the marinade over heat and adding a bit of smoky char and flavor."

# Grilled and Chilled Shrimp and Crab

**SERVES 6**

2 cloves garlic, sliced

8 fresh basil leaves, julienned

4 fresh flat-leaf parsley sprigs, chopped

1 tablespoon paprika

4 tablespoons extra virgin olive oil

18 jumbo shrimp, peeled and deveined

12 cooked snow crab claws

Salt and freshly ground black pepper

Cocktail sauce for serving

**To marinate the seafood:** In a large bowl, whisk together the garlic, basil, parsley, paprika, and olive oil. Add the shrimp and crab and toss to coat the shellfish evenly. Cover and marinate overnight in the refrigerator.

**To grill the seafood:** At least 2 to 3 hours or as many as 12 hours before serving, preheat a gas grill to medium-high, or light a fire in a charcoal grill and let it burn just until the coals are covered with gray ash and very hot.

Remove the shellfish from the marinade, and season with salt and pepper. Set the shrimp and crab claws on the grill grate. Cook the shrimp, turning once, until pink, curled, and just cooked through, 2 to 3 minutes per side. Grill the crab claws, turning once, until heated through, about 1 minute per side

**To chill and serve:** Transfer the shrimp and crab to a rimmed baking sheet and let cool to room temperature, then refrigerate for at least 2 hours. Serve chilled with your favorite cocktail sauce. You can either divide the seafood among individual serving plates and garnish each plate with a dollop of cocktail sauce, or you can arrange the seafood on a platter and pass the cocktail sauce at the table.

# Grilled Squid in Herb Butter

"My uncle from Venice used to deep-fry seafood and toss it in a garlicky herb butter. This squid is based on that idea, but it's grilled, not fried, so it's lighter and more flavorful."

**SERVES 6**

2 pounds cleaned squid bodies and tentacles

½ cup olive oil

1 clove garlic, minced

¼ cup plus 2 tablespoons chopped fresh flat-leaf parsley

Juice of 1 lemon

½ cup butter, at room temperature

2 tablespoons chopped fresh basil

2 tablespoons chopped fresh thyme

2 tablespoons chopped fresh chives

Salt and freshly ground black pepper

2 lemons, cut into wedges

Crusty bread for serving

**To marinate the squid:** Slice the squid bodies into ½-inch-wide rings. In a medium bowl, combine the squid rings and tentacles, olive oil, garlic, ¼ cup of the parsley, and the lemon juice and toss to coat evenly. Cover and refrigerate overnight.

**To grill the squid:** Preheat a gas grill to medium-high, preheat a stove-top grill pan over medium-high heat, or light a fire in a charcoal grill and let it burn just until the coals are covered with gray ash and very hot.

While the grill or grill pan is heating, make the herb butter: In a food processor, combine the butter, basil, thyme, chives, and the remaining 2 tablespoons parsley. Pulse to blend the butter with the herbs. Transfer to a large bowl and reserve at room temperature.

Remove the squid rings and tentacles from the marinade and season with salt and pepper. Place the squid pieces directly on the grill grate or grill pan. If the bars on the grate are widely spaced, use a grill basket or screen. Grill, turning once, until the flesh begins to char and curl, about 2 minutes per side.

As soon as the squid pieces are ready, quickly transfer them to the bowl with the herb butter and toss to melt the butter and coat the squid, (This may need to be done in batches, depending on the size of your grill or grill pan.) Season to taste with salt and pepper.

Mound the squid on a platter or divide among 6 individual serving plates. Garnish with the lemon wedges and serve immediately. Pass the bread at the table for soaking up the butter sauce.

# Spaghetti and Shellfish

"If you're good at juggling pots and pans, you can back-time this so the seafood and pasta are ready at the same time. Or, just keep the sautéed seafood warm while you cook the spaghetti. Either way, you'll have an authentic *frutti di mare* pasta with the added holiday luxury of lobster."

**SERVES 6**

4 cups water

1 tablespoon salt, plus more to season

24 littleneck clams, scrubbed

¼ cup extra virgin olive oil, plus more for serving (optional)

2 cloves garlic, thinly sliced

1 small leek, including light green part, or onion, diced

14 cherry tomatoes, halved

¼ cup dry white wine

Freshly ground black pepper

24 PEI mussels, scrubbed and debearded

1 pound spaghetti

2 pounds cooked lobster meat, roughly chopped or cut into chunks, at room temperature

8 fresh basil leaves, cut into strips

4 fresh flat-leaf parsley sprigs, chopped

In a large bowl, combine the water and 1 tablespoon salt and stir to dissolve the salt. Add the clams and soak at room temperature for 20 minutes to purge them of grit. Drain and rinse the clams before proceeding.

Bring a large pot three-fourths full of salted water to a boil.

Meanwhile, heat the olive oil in a large skillet over medium heat until it shimmers. Add the garlic and leek and sauté until tender, 3 to 4 minutes. Add the clams, cherry tomatoes, wine, a pinch of salt, and a grind of pepper, then cover the pan and simmer for 8 minutes. Add the mussels, re-cover, and simmer until all of the shellfish are open, 2 to 3 minutes longer. Remove and discard any shellfish that failed to open. Taste the cooking liquid and adjust the seasoning with salt and pepper if needed. Move the skillet to a warm place while you cook the spaghetti.

Add the spaghetti to the boiling water and cook until al dente, according to package directions. Scoop out and reserve 1 cup of the cooking water, then drain the pasta in a colander.

Transfer the pasta to a large bowl, add the lobster meat, the clams and mussels and their cooking liquid, the basil, and the parsley and toss to combine. Season with salt and pepper. Add some of the reserved cooking water if the pasta seems too dry. Drizzle with additional olive oil, if desired, and serve immediately.

**TODD'S TIP:** PEI (Prince Edward Island) mussels from the Atlantic north of Nova Scotia are widely available and consistently plump and tasty.

"This classic Italian dessert makes a simple, satisfying conclusion to a big meal with a lot of flavors. Top it with a good-quality chocolate or orange sauce, or try it New England style with a drizzle of warm maple syrup."

# Semolina Pudding

**SERVES 6 TO 8**

4 cups whole milk

1 cup sugar

½ vanilla bean

1 cinnamon stick

¾ cup semolina

Grated zest of 1 orange

½ cup butter, cut into small cubes

5 large eggs

2 large egg whites

Butter, at room temperature, or nonstick cooking spray for the foil

Chocolate or orange sauce for serving

Preheat the oven to 350°F.

In a large, heavy bottomed saucepan, bring the milk just to a boil over medium-high heat, then remove from the heat. Stir in the sugar, vanilla bean, and cinnamon stick and let steep for 20 minutes.

Remove the cinnamon stick and vanilla bean from the milk mixture and discard the cinnamon stick. When the vanilla bean is cool enough to handle, using a sharp paring knife, split the bean lengthwise. Then, using the tip of the knife, scrape the seeds from the pod into the milk mixture and discard the pod. Return the saucepan to medium heat, bring the mixture to a simmer, and slowly whisk in the semolina and orange zest. Continue to whisk until thickened to the consistency of a thin batter, about 5 minutes. Remove from the heat and stir in the butter.

In a medium bowl, whisk the 5 whole eggs until blended. Add 2 cups of the hot semolina mixture, a little at a time, while whisking constantly. Then whisk the egg-semolina mixture into the semolina remaining in the saucepan until thoroughly combined.

In a large bowl, using a clean whisk or a handheld mixer on medium-high speed, whip the egg whites until stiff peaks form. Gradually fold the semolina mixture into the egg whites. Pour into a 9-by-13-inch baking dish. Butter one side of a sheet of aluminum foil large enough to cover the baking dish, or spray one side with nonstick spray. Cover the baking dish with the foil, coated side down. (The pudding will rise during baking and some of it may touch the foil; the coating will prevent sticking.)

Place the covered baking dish in a large roasting pan. Open the oven door and pull out the center oven rack most of the way, but not so far that it will tip when the pan is set on it. Set the pan holding the baking dish on the rack and pour hot water into the roasting pan to a depth of 1 inch. Slowly slide the rack into the oven, and close the oven door. Bake for 20 minutes, then open a corner of the foil and continue to bake until the pudding is just set in the middle when tested with a knife, 15 to 20 minutes longer.

Remove the baking dish from the water bath, uncover, and spoon the warm pudding into individual serving bowls or plates. Serve with your favorite chocolate sauce.

MARCUS SAMUELSSON

# AN AMERICAN JULBORD

Marcus grew up in Sweden and has happy memories of the greatest Swedish meal of all, the *julbord* (think "yule" plus "smorgasbord"), an abundant spread of hot and cold dishes, including plenty of cured fish, meatballs, pickles, breads, and cheeses. Here in the US, he adds creative touches inspired by Mexico, Asia, Africa, and his own fertile imagination.

"Here's my recipe for the traditional Swedish infused vodka known as aquavit. Enjoy it with soda water or on the rocks, garnished, if you like, with a piece of the infused fruit."

## Citrus-Infused Vodka

**MAKES 2 QUARTS**

1-inch piece fresh ginger, peeled

2 kaffir lime leaves

¼ cup sugar

½ cup water

2 limes

1 pink grapefruit

1 orange

1 lemon

2 quarts potato-based vodka

In a small saucepan, combine the ginger, lime leaves, sugar, and water and bring to a boil over high heat, stirring to dissolve the sugar. Remove from the heat and let cool to room temperature.

Cut each lime into 6 wedges. Cut the grapefruit, orange, and lemon into thin slices. Divide the fruit evenly between two 2-quart glass jars. Divide the ginger-sugar syrup and the vodka evenly between the jars. Cover tightly and store at room temperature for 3 weeks.

Strain the contents of both jars through a fine-mesh sieve, then transfer the strained liquid to bottles. Cap tightly and store in a cool cupboard. Serve well chilled.

# Gravlax with Purple Mustard

"Gravlax—Swedish home-cured salmon—is easy to make from just five ingredients: sugar, salt, pepper, dill, and salmon. It's usually eaten with mustard, and that's where I like to get creative—like this beautiful version that gets its vivid color from reduced red wine and port."

## SERVES 10 TO 12

1 cup sugar

½ cup kosher salt

2 tablespoons freshly cracked white peppercorns

1 skin-on salmon fillet in one piece, 2½ to 3 pounds

2 to 3 large bunches fresh dill, coarsely chopped

Purple Mustard (see right)

Boiled Fingerling Potatoes with Salmon Roe Vinaigrette (page 138)

In a small bowl, stir together the sugar, salt, and peppercorns, mixing well. To remove any pin bones from the salmon, place the fillet, skin side down, on a clean work surface. Run your fingertips over the surface and, using kitchen tweezers, remove any pin bones you find, making sure to pull them out in the direction they point. Place the salmon in a shallow dish and rub a handful of the sugar mixture into each side of the fillet. Sprinkle the salmon with the remaining sugar mixture and cover with the dill.

Cover the dish and let stand in a cool spot for 6 hours. Then transfer the dish to the refrigerator and let the salmon cure in the refrigerator for 36 hours.

Remove the salmon from the dish and carefully scrape off all the seasoning. Pat the fish dry with paper towels and transfer to a cutting board. Slice the salmon as thinly as possible against the grain, cutting the slices away from the skin. Arrange the slices on a platter and serve with the mustard and fingerling potatoes.

## Purple Mustard

MAKES ABOUT 2 CUPS

2 cups dry red wine

1 cup ruby port or Madeira

2 shallots, finely chopped

2 tablespoons mustard seeds (preferably purple)

4 white peppercorns

Leaves from 2 fresh tarragon sprigs

1 cup Dijon mustard

1 teaspoon Colman's mustard powder

In a saucepan, combine the red wine, port, shallots, mustard seeds, peppercorns, and tarragon and bring to a boil over medium-high heat. Boil gently until reduced to ½ cup, about 30 minutes.

Remove from the heat, transfer to a blender, add the Dijon mustard and mustard powder, and process until smooth. Let cool, transfer to a jar with a tight-fitting lid, and refrigerate until serving. The mustard will keep in the refrigerator for up to 2 months.

# Boiled Fingerling Potatoes
## with Salmon Roe Vinaigrette

"Boiled potatoes are a classic accompaniment to a platter of gravlax. I like to balance the mild creaminess of fingerlings with a sweet-spicy Asian-style salmon roe vinaigrette that makes the perfect bridge to the flavor of the cured fish." (photo page 136)

**SERVES 8 TO 10**

1½ pounds fingerling potatoes

2 tablespoons salt

2 tablespoons chopped fresh dill fronds, stems reserved

¼ cup olive oil

2 teaspoons *shichimi togarashi* (Japanese spice powder)

2 tablespoons mirin

1 teaspoon wasabi paste

¼ cup soy sauce

2 tablespoons salmon roe

¼ cup plain yogurt

In a saucepan, combine the potatoes, salt, and dill stems with water to cover and bring to a boil over high heat. Reduce the heat to medium and simmer until the potatoes are tender when pierced with a fork, about 15 minutes.

Drain the potatoes and discard the dill stems. Cut the warm potatoes in half lengthwise and transfer to a serving bowl. Add the olive oil and *shichimi togarashi* and stir to mix. Let cool to room temperature.

In a small bowl, stir together the mirin, wasabi, soy sauce, and salmon roe. Pour the mirin mixture over the potatoes, stir gently to combine, and then transfer to a serving bowl. Sprinkle the chopped dill over the potatoes. Spoon the yogurt in a dollop on top for garnish and serve.

# Helga's Meatballs

"Like gravlax, these meatballs, served with lingonberry preserves, pickles, and mashed potatoes, are a Swedish institution. They were one of the first things I learned to make, and this version is based on my grandmother Helga's recipe."

**MAKES ABOUT 24 MEATBALLS**

**PICKLED CUCUMBERS**

2 English cucumbers

1 cup distilled white vinegar

1 cup water

¼ cup sugar

2 tablespoons kosher salt

1 teaspoon yellow mustard seeds

1 teaspoon red pepper flakes

4 allspice berries

**MEATBALLS**

½ cup fine dried bread crumbs

¼ cup heavy cream

2 tablespoons olive oil

1 red onion, finely chopped

8 ounces ground beef chuck or sirloin

8 ounces ground veal

8 ounces ground pork

2 tablespoons honey

1 large egg

Kosher salt and freshly ground black pepper

3 tablespoons unsalted butter

**SAUCE**

1 cup chicken broth

½ cup heavy cream

¼ cup lingonberry preserves

2 tablespoons pickle juice from Pickled Cucumbers (above)

Kosher salt and freshly ground black pepper

Lingonberry preserves for serving

**For the pickled cucumbers:** Trim off the ends of the cucumbers, then, using a mandoline or a sharp knife, thinly slice them. Place the slices in a large, heatproof bowl.

In a saucepan, combine the vinegar, water, sugar, salt, mustard seeds, pepper flakes, and allspice over high heat and bring to a boil, stirring to dissolve the sugar. Boil for 1 minute to ensure the sugar is fully dissolved. Remove from the heat and pour over the cucumbers. The cucumbers should be fully immersed. Let cool to room temperature, then cover and refrigerate for up to 3 days before serving (if you can wait that long).

**For the meatballs:** In a small bowl, combine the bread crumbs and cream and stir with a fork until the crumbs are evenly moistened. Set aside.

In a small skillet, heat the olive oil over medium heat. Add the onion and sauté until softened, about 5 minutes. Remove from the heat and let cool to room temperature.

In a large bowl, combine the beef, veal, pork, cooled onion, honey, and egg and mix well with your hands. Season with salt and pepper, then add the bread crumb–cream mixture and mix well. Lightly moisten a large plate with water. With wet hands (to keep the mixture from sticking), shape the mixture into balls the size of a golf ball and place them on the moistened plate. You should have about 24 meatballs.

In a large skillet, melt the butter over medium-high heat. Working in batches, add the meatballs and cook, turning frequently, until nicely browned on all sides and cooked through, 7 to 8 minutes. Transfer the meatballs to a plate and set aside. Pour off all but 1 tablespoon of the fat from the skillet and reserve the skillet for making the sauce.

**For the sauce:** Return the skillet to medium-high heat, whisk in the broth, cream, lingonberry preserves, and pickle juice, and bring to a simmer. Season with salt and pepper.

Add the meatballs to the sauce, reduce the heat to medium, and simmer until the sauce thickens slightly and the meatballs are heated through, about 5 minutes. Transfer the meatballs and their sauce to a deep serving platter. Serve the pickled cucumbers and extra lingonberry preserves on the side.

# Chorizo-Style Meatballs
## with Tomatillo-Avocado Salsa

**MAKES ABOUT 24 MEATBALLS**

### TOMATILLO-AVOCADO SALSA

3 tablespoons extra virgin olive oil

2 cloves garlic, minced

1 serrano chile, seeded, if desired, and finely chopped

1 shallot, finely chopped

2 tomatillos, papery husks removed and finely chopped

1 ripe avocado, halved, pitted, peeled, and cubed

1 small red onion, finely chopped

1 jalapeño chile, seeded, if desired, and finely chopped

Juice of 1 lime

2 fresh cilantro sprigs, chopped

4 drops Tabasco sauce

1 teaspoon salt

Freshly ground black pepper

### MEATBALLS

12 ounces ground lamb

12 ounces ground pork

3 cloves garlic, minced

1½ teaspoons mild chili powder

1½ teaspoons salt

¾ teaspoon ground cumin

1½ teaspoons dried oregano, rubbed between fingertips

1½ teaspoons smoked paprika

Freshly ground black pepper

3 tablespoons olive oil

**For the salsa:** In a sauté pan, heat the olive oil over high heat. Add the garlic, serrano chile, and shallot and sauté until fragrant, about 2 minutes. Add the tomatillos and sauté until softened, another 3 minutes. Transfer to a medium bowl and let cool completely.

With a rubber spatula, fold the avocado, onion, jalapeño chile, lime juice, cilantro, and Tabasco into the cooled tomatillo mixture. Season with the salt and pepper. Cover with plastic wrap, pressing it directly onto the surface of the salsa (this will keep the avocado from browning), and refrigerate until serving.

**For the meatballs:** In a large bowl, combine the lamb, pork, garlic, chili powder, salt, cumin, oregano, paprika, and a few grinds of pepper and mix well with your hands. Lightly moisten a large plate with water. With wet hands (to keep the mixture from sticking), shape the mixture into balls the size of a golf ball and place them on the moistened plate. You should have about 24 meatballs.

In a large sauté pan, heat the olive oil over medium-high heat. Working in batches, add the meatballs and cook, turning frequently, until nicely browned on all sides and cooked through, 7 to 8 minutes. Using a slotted spoon, transfer to paper towels to drain briefly.

Arrange the meatballs on a platter and serve right away, with the salsa on the side.

"These make a fun contrast in flavor and color to the Swedish meatballs. They taste a lot like fresh Mexican chorizo, especially when you serve them with my chunky guacamole-style salsa."

# Ripped Pork

"I created this meltingly tender slow-cooked pork for Red Rooster, where we do what I call 'elevated American comfort food' with international flavors. Serve it alongside the Pickled Cabbage with some good soft rolls for sandwich making."

**SERVES 8 TO 10**

1 teaspoon cumin seeds

1 teaspoon fennel seeds

1 teaspoon coriander seeds

1 tablespoon chili powder

1 tablespoon smoked paprika

¼ cup tomato paste

1 cup tamarind paste

10 prunes, pitted

2 cups bourbon

3 cups chicken broth, plus more if needed

8 pounds boneless Boston butt

Preheat the oven to 250°F.

In a spice grinder, combine the cumin, fennel, and coriander seeds and grind to a fine powder. Transfer to a large bowl and stir in the chili powder, paprika, tomato paste, tamarind paste, prunes, bourbon, and broth to make a braising liquid.

Put the pork in a large Dutch oven or roasting pan and pour the braising liquid over the top. Place in the oven, uncovered, and cook, basting every 30 minutes with the braising liquid and adding additional broth if needed to keep the pork about three-fourths submerged, until fork-tender, about 8 hours.

Remove from the oven, transfer the pork to a cutting board, and let cool for 5 to 10 minutes. Carefully ladle off the fat from the top of the braising liquid and discard. Taste the braising liquid and adjust with salt and pepper if needed.

Using 2 forks, pull the pork into coarse shreds and place in a bowl. Gradually add the braising liquid to the pork until the pork is very moist but still holds together. You may not need all of the braising liquid. Taste for seasoning and adjust with salt and pepper if needed. Reheat, if necessary, and serve warm.

# Pickled Cabbage

"With the buttery richness of slow-cooked pork, I want something cool, spicy, tangy, and crunchy. This North African–inspired slaw is just the ticket."

**SERVES 8 TO 10**

2 grapefruits

1 cup white wine vinegar

½ cup soy sauce

2 cups water

1 cup sugar

1 large red onion, thinly sliced

4 cloves garlic, minced

½ cup dry-roasted peanuts, coarsely chopped

2 tablespoons peanut oil

2 teaspoons *harissa* (North African hot sauce)

1 head napa cabbage, cored and shredded (about 16 cups)

Leaves from 4 fresh basil sprigs, chopped

4 fresh cilantro sprigs, chopped

4-inch piece fresh ginger, peeled and grated

Cut a thin slice off the top and bottom of each grapefruit to reveal the flesh. Stand 1 grapefruit upright on a cutting board. Using a sharp knife and following the contour of the fruit, cut downward to remove the peel and pith. Holding the peeled grapefruit over a bowl, cut along both sides of each segment to free it from the membrane, catching the segments and any juice in the bowl. Repeat with the remaining grapefruit. Set aside.

In a medium saucepan, combine the vinegar, soy sauce, water, and sugar and bring to a boil over high heat, stirring to dissolve the sugar. Transfer to a large heatproof bowl and let cool.

Add the onion, garlic, peanuts, peanut oil, and *harissa* to the cooled vinegar mixture and mix well. Put the cabbage in a deep baking dish or a large bowl and pour the cooled peanut-onion mixture over the top. Toss to combine. Cover and let stand for 10 minutes to allow the flavors to blend.

Drain the cabbage mixture in a colander and transfer to a large bowl. Add the grapefruit segments and juice, basil, cilantro, and ginger and toss gently to mix well. Serve immediately.

## MING TSAI

# DUMPLING PARTY

---

When Ming was a kid, his extended family—fourteen people, three generations—would gather around the ping-pong table for an afternoon of pot sticker and spring roll making. They'd feast on the dumplings for dinner and then wrap up the evening with a rousing game of mahjong. Here's how to turn that idea into a fun holiday party at your place.

# Blue Ginger House Slaw

"If you're making a meal of dumplings, you've got to have something fresh and crunchy in the mix. This colorful slaw, with its soy-mustard vinaigrette, will do the trick." (photo page 146)

**SERVES 10**

3 cups finely sliced napa cabbage (⅛-inch-wide ribbons)

3 cups finely sliced red cabbage (⅛-inch-wide ribbons)

¾ cup shredded carrots

1 bunch scallions, tender green parts only, thinly sliced

¼ cup whole-grain mustard

¼ cup minced shallots

3 tablespoons rice vinegar

1 tablespoon naturally brewed organic soy sauce or tamari

1½ teaspoons sugar

¼ cup grape seed oil or canola oil

Kosher salt and freshly ground pepper

In a large bowl, combine the cabbages, carrots, and scallions, toss to mix, and set aside.

In a blender, combine the mustard, shallots, vinegar, soy sauce, and sugar and process until smooth. With the blender running, slowly drizzle in the oil and process until the vinaigrette emulsifies. Taste and adjust the seasoning with salt and pepper if needed.

Add half of the vinaigrette to the cabbage mixture and stir and toss to mix well. Taste the slaw and add more vinaigrette as needed. You may not need all of the vinaigrette. Serve immediately or within 1 hour.

# Two Dipping Sauces (photo page 146)

### Dim Sum Dipper

"This is basically what I always make from the tabletop condiments at a dim sum house: you mix up a dab of chile-garlic sauce with a little vinegar, soy, and sesame oil and you're set."

MAKES ABOUT 1 CUP

2 tablespoons *sambal oelek* (Southeast Asian chile paste)

½ cup rice vinegar

½ cup soy sauce

1 teaspoon Asian sesame oil

3 scallions, including tender green parts, thinly sliced

In a small bowl, stir together the chile paste, vinegar, soy sauce, sesame oil, and scallions. Use immediately, or cover and refrigerate for up to 4 days (in which case, add the scallions just before serving).

### Sweet Chile Dipping Sauce

"This is my punched-up version of the classic sweet-hot Thai dipping sauce for grilled chicken."

MAKES ABOUT 1½ CUPS

1 roasted red bell pepper

1¼ cups Mae Ploy brand sweet chile sauce

1 tablespoon *sambal oelek* (Southeast Asian chile paste)

Kosher salt

In a blender, combine the roasted pepper, sweet chile sauce, chile paste, and a pinch of salt and process until smooth. Pour through a fine-mesh sieve placed over a bowl to remove any seeds. Taste and adjust the seasoning with salt. Use immediately, or cover and refrigerate for up to 4 days.

# Handmade Dumplings Three Ways

Mix and match is the principle here. You've got three great dumpling fillings, each of which will fill one batch of Hot-Water Dough Dumpling Wrappers. Make one, two, or all three fillings the night before your party so the flavors come together and there's less prep work for your guests. Make the dough (scaling up the recipe so you have one batch per type of filling) once the guests arrive, so it's fresh and springy. Or, to save time, you can buy round *gyoza* or pot sticker wrappers. If you're making more than one kind of dumpling, you can follow the directions to pan sear some, steam some, and boil some all at the same time.

## Traditional Pork and Ginger

"This classic pot sticker filling, with its rich pork flavor simply accented with ginger and scallions, is my family's house recipe."

1 cup finely shredded cabbage

2 teaspoons kosher salt, plus more to season

1 pound ground pork

¼ cup minced, peeled fresh ginger

1½ teaspoons Asian sesame oil

½ cup thinly sliced scallions (white and tender green parts)

Freshly ground black pepper

Put the cabbage in a sieve placed over a bowl. Sprinkle the cabbage with the 2 teaspoons salt and let stand for 30 minutes. Rinse the cabbage, drain well, and then chop finely.

Prepare a large ice bath. Set a medium bowl over the ice bath. In another medium bowl, combine the cabbage, pork, ginger, and sesame oil and mix well. Fold in the scallions and season with salt and pepper. In a small sauté pan or in a microwave, cook a small nugget of the filling, then taste and adjust the seasoning if needed.

## Black Bean and Shrimp

"The French trick of adding frozen butter gives this filling a springy, mousselike consistency. Chop the butter into small cubes, then freeze it for about an hour."

Canola oil for sautéing

1 tablespoon fermented black beans, rinsed, drained, and minced

1 tablespoon minced, peeled fresh ginger

1 bunch scallions, including tender green parts, thinly sliced

1½ pounds shrimp, peeled and deveined

2 large eggs

4 tablespoons butter, cut into ⅛-inch dice and frozen

Kosher salt and freshly ground pepper

Heat a wok or sauté pan over medium-high heat. When the pan is hot, pour in enough canola oil to film the bottom of the pan lightly, and then swirl to coat evenly with the oil. Add the black beans, ginger, and scallions and cook, stirring constantly, until fragrant, 1 to 2 minutes. Remove from the heat and transfer to a medium bowl. Set aside to cool.

In a food processor, combine the shrimp and eggs and process until almost smooth. Add the butter and pulse briefly until incorporated but still visible in small pieces. Season with salt and pepper.

Fold the shrimp mixture into the cooled black bean mixture. In a small sauté pan or in a microwave, cook a small nugget of the filling, then taste and adjust the seasoning if needed.

## Vegetarian Shiitake and Leek

"Thanks to the rich flavor of shiitake mushrooms, these can go head to head with any meat-filled dumpling out there."

3½ ounces bean thread noodles

Canola oil for sautéing

2 tablespoons minced garlic

2 tablespoons minced, peeled fresh ginger

4 serrano chiles, finely chopped

1 cup hoisin sauce

4 cups thinly sliced shiitake mushroom caps

4 large leeks, white part only, cut into matchsticks

Kosher salt and freshly ground pepper

1 cup chopped fresh cilantro

2 cups chopped scallions (white and tender green parts)

In a bowl, soak the noodles in warm water to cover until soft, 10 to 15 minutes. Drain well, measure out 2 cups, and cut into 2-inch lengths. Set aside.

Heat a wok or sauté pan over high heat. When the pan is hot, pour in enough canola oil to film the bottom of the pan lightly, and then swirl to coat evenly with the oil. Add the garlic, ginger, and chiles and cook, stirring constantly, until soft, about 2 minutes. Do not allow the aromatics to burn. Reduce the heat to medium, add the hoisin sauce, and cook, stirring, until it loses its raw bean taste, about 3 minutes. Add the mushrooms and leeks and cook, stirring, until soft, about 6 minutes. Season with salt and pepper, then transfer the mixture to a sieve placed over a bowl. Using a large spoon, press against the mixture to force out the excess moisture. Let cool completely.

## Hot-Water Dough Dumpling Wrappers

MAKES ABOUT 70 WRAPPERS

4 cups all-purpose flour, plus more for kneading and dusting

½ teaspoon salt

2 cups boiling water

**FOR SHAPING**

1 large egg

2 tablespoons water

**To mix the dough by hand:** In a large heatproof bowl, stir together the flour and salt. Add the boiling water in ¼-cup increments and mix with chopsticks until a ball forms and the dough is no longer too hot to handle. You may not need all of the water. Turn the dough out onto a lightly floured work surface and knead until smooth and elastic, 15 to 20 minutes. If the dough feels sticky as you knead, mix in more flour 1 tablespoon at a time. Shape the dough into a disk, wrap tightly with plastic wrap, and let rest at room temperature for 1 hour.

**To mix the dough in a stand mixer:** In the bowl of a stand mixer fitted with the dough hook, stir together the flour and salt. On low speed, gradually add the boiling water until the flour mixture is evenly moistened and forms a ball. The dough should not be sticky. If it is sticky, mix in more flour 1 tablespoon at a time. Very lightly flour a work surface, place the dough on it, and bring the dough together into a disk. Wrap tightly with plastic wrap and let rest at room temperature for 1 hour.

**To roll out the wrappers:** Liberally flour the work surface and place the dough on it. Divide the dough in half and leave one-half covered. Shape the other half into a log, then roll it back and forth under your palms into a rope about 1 inch in diameter and 18 inches long. Cut the rope into about 35 ½-inch pieces. Stand 1 piece on end, flatten it with your palm, and, using a lightly dusted rolling pin, roll out the dough into a circle about 3 inches in diameter and 1/16 thick. (You can also use a tortilla press to make the dough circles.) Roll the edges of the dough circle a little thinner than the center, so when you double them over around the filling, they will be the same thickness as the rest of the wrapper. Repeat with 4 more dough pieces, then fill the 5 wrappers as directed below. Roll out and fill the remaining dough pieces the same way, and then repeat with the remaining half of the dough.

It is important to roll out only 5 wrappers at a time and fill them right away because the wrappers dry out quickly and they cannot be stacked without sticking to one another. If possible, recruit a coworker, so that one of you can roll out the wrappers and the other can fill them.

In a small bowl, whisk together the egg and water to make a wash. Have ready 2 baking sheets very lightly dusted with flour or 2 nonstick baking or cookie sheets.

**To form the dumplings:** Lay 5 wrappers on a work surface. Place 1½ teaspoons of the filling in the center of each wrapper. Avoid getting any filling on the edges of a wrapper, which would prevent it from sealing properly. With a finger or pastry brush, paint the circumference of each wrapper with the egg wash. Fold each wrapper in half to form a half-moon, then press the edges together to seal. Holding the dumpling in one hand, and starting at the center of the curved edge, make 3 evenly placed pleats, working toward the bottom-right corner. Again starting at the center of the curve, make 3 more pleats, working toward the bottom-left corner. Press the bottom of the dumpling gently on the work surface to flatten it so it will stand upright. As the dumplings are formed, set them on the prepared baking sheets. Cook them in one of the following ways.

**To pan sear the dumplings:** Heat a large, nonstick lidded sauté pan over high heat. When the pan is hot, add about 2 tablespoons canola oil and swirl to coat the pan bottom. When the oil is hot, arrange the dumplings, flattened bottoms down, in 2 or 3 rows of 5 dumplings each. Cook the dumplings without disturbing them until the bottoms are browned, 3 to 4 minutes. Add about ½ cup water and immediately cover the pan to avoid splattering. Lift the cover and make sure the water in the pan is about ⅛ inch deep. If it isn't, add more water as needed. Re-cover the pan and cook the dumplings until they are puffy yet firm and the water has evaporated, 8 to 10 minutes. If the water evaporates before the dumplings are done, add more water in ¼-cup

increments. If the dumplings appear done but water remains in the pan, drain off as much water as possible and return the pan uncovered to high heat to evaporate any remaining liquid. Continue to cook uncovered until the bottoms of the dumplings are once again crisp, 2 to 3 minutes. Be careful they do not burn. Transfer the dumplings to a platter.

**To steam the dumplings:** Use two 12-inch stacking bamboo steamer baskets with a lid and a wok with its lid. Place 1 basket in the wok. Add water to the wok, filling to ½ inch below the bottom of the steamer basket (once the water is boiling, it must not touch the basket). Remove the basket from the wok, cover the wok, and bring the water to a boil over high heat. Oil the racks of both steamer baskets with canola oil. Arrange the dumplings, flattened bottoms down, in 2 or 3 rows of 5 dumplings each, making sure the dumplings do not touch. Stack the steamer baskets in the wok over the boiling water and reduce the heat to medium. Cover the top basket and steam the dumplings until the filling feels firm when a dumpling is pressed with a fingertip, about 12 minutes. Remove the baskets from the wok and transfer the dumplings to a platter.

**To boil the dumplings:** Bring a large pot three-fourths full of water to a boil over high heat. Working quickly, add 12 or 15 dumplings, one at a time, and then immediately stir them gently so they don't stick together. Bring the water back to a boil, and as soon as the dumplings start to float to the top, add ½ cup cold water (the cold water slows down the cooking process, which allows the filling to cook and keeps the water from boiling so hard that the dumplings break apart). Once the dumplings start to float again, taste one to see if it is done. If not, add another ½ cup cold water and wait until the dumplings float again. When the dumplings are ready, using a slotted spoon or a skimmer, transfer them to a platter, being careful that they do not touch or they will stick together.

"A granita is about the easiest frozen dessert you can make. It takes no time to put together, and you don't even need an ice-cream freezer."

# Pineapple-Champagne Granita

"You'll use most of the bottle of Champagne to make this recipe. Save the rest to pour into each serving dish the next day. If it's a bit flat, that's fine—you're only adding a splash. You can also make the granita with sparkling cider for kids and nondrinkers."

**SERVES 10**

1 pineapple

2 cups Champagne, *cava*, or other sparkling wine, plus remainder of bottle for serving

¼ cup honey

2 tablespoons crushed pink peppercorns

Cut off the leafy crown and the base of the pineapple. Stand the pineapple upright and cut away the skin in long, vertical strips, leaving the small, prickly "eyes" on the flesh. Lay the pineapple on its side and, working in a spiral pattern, cut shallow furrows to remove the eyes. Cut the pineapple lengthwise into 8 wedges, cut away and discard the core from each wedge, and then coarsely chop the wedges

In a food processor, combine the pineapple and 2 cups Champagne and process until smooth. Taste for sweetness, then add the honey, a little at a time, until you reach the desired sweetness. You may not need all of the honey.

Pour the purée into a square or rectangular container at least 2 inches deep and freeze overnight. Put the bottle with the remaining Champagne in the refrigerator at the same time. At least 1 hour before serving, chill 10 martini glasses or serving cups.

To serve, using a large fork, scrape the pineapple mixture to create large flakes. Divide the chilled Champagne evenly among the chilled glasses or cups. Spoon the granita on top, dividing it equally. Garnish with the pink peppercorns and serve immediately.

## MICHELLE BERNSTEIN
# HANUKKAH DINNER

Michelle grew up celebrating Hanukkah. "Well, not so much the holiday," she clarifies. "We celebrated the eating part." That meant a little candle lighting, a little gift exchanging, and a lot of food—all homemade, with a mix of family favorites and new ideas. That's the spirit of her warmly traditional yet decidedly contemporary Hanukkah menu.

# Butter Lettuce and Shaved Fennel Salad

"Let's be honest, Hanukkah is all about frying. That's what this crisp, refreshing salad is doing here. Its fresh, lemony flavor will cut through the fat and wake up your palate."

**SERVES 6 TO 8**

1 large head butter lettuce, separated into leaves

1 fennel bulb, trimmed and shaved as thinly as possible on a mandoline or with a sharp knife

1 cup oil-cured black olives, pitted

1 head Belgian endive, leaves separated

4 ounces Manchego cheese, grated on the largest holes on a box grater

½ cup fresh tarragon leaves

**DRESSING**

2 tablespoons plus 1½ teaspoons fresh lemon juice

6 tablespoons olive oil

Kosher salt and freshly ground pepper

In a large salad bowl, combine the lettuce, fennel, olives, endive, Manchego, and tarragon and set aside. To make the dressing, put the lemon juice in a small bowl. Slowly whisk the olive oil into the lemon juice to form an emulsion. Season with salt and pepper. Pour the dressing over the salad and toss to coat evenly.

# French Bean and Pearl Onion Ragout

"These crisp-tender beans and sweet pearl onions would be right at home at any holiday meal, especially Thanksgiving. It's easy to peel pearl onions. Just throw them into boiling water for a minute, and then drain them and pop them out of their skins."

**SERVES 6 TO 8**

1 pound French beans, trimmed

2 tablespoons butter

1 tablespoon olive oil

8 ounces pearl onions, peeled and trimmed

½ teaspoon sugar

¼ teaspoon kosher salt, plus more to season

¾ cup chicken broth

½ teaspoon finely chopped fresh thyme

¼ cup chopped fresh flat-leaf parsley

Freshly ground black pepper

Bring a large pot three-fourths full of salted water to a rolling boil over high heat. While the water is heating, prepare an ice bath.

Add the beans to the boiling water and cook just until crisp-tender, about 1½ minutes. Drain the beans and immediately plunge them into the ice bath to halt the cooking and set the color. Drain the beans and dry them thoroughly in a clean kitchen towel or with paper towels. Set aside.

In a large sauté pan, melt the butter with the olive oil over medium heat until the butter melts and foams. Add the pearl onions and cook, shaking the pan occasionally, for 4 minutes. Sprinkle the sugar and the ¼ teaspoon salt over the onions and cook, shaking the pan occasionally, until the onions are golden brown, about 2 minutes. Add the broth, raise the heat to high, and bring to a boil. Boil until the broth is reduced to a thick syrup, about 5 minutes.

Add the reserved beans, thyme, and parsley and toss until the beans are heated through. Season with salt and pepper. Transfer to a warmed platter and serve immediately.

# Scallion Potato Pancakes

"Fried foods like potato pancakes (a.k.a. *latkes*) and doughnuts are traditional for Hanukkah because the holiday celebrates the famous miracle of the oil that lasted eight days. For a nice little party appetizer, make bite-sized pancakes and top them with crème fraîche and caviar or smoked salmon, whitefish, or trout."

**MAKES 14 TO 16 PANCAKES;
SERVES 6 TO 8**

2 pounds Yukon Gold potatoes, peeled and halved

1 yellow onion, cut into 6 to 8 pieces

1 large egg, lightly beaten

6 scallions, including tender green parts, thinly sliced

2 tablespoons all-purpose flour

1 teaspoon salt

½ cup vegetable oil, plus more if needed

Applesauce and sour cream for serving

**For the batter:** In a food processor fitted with the grater attachment, grate the potatoes and onion. Transfer the mixture to a colander and press down firmly to remove all the excess liquid. Then transfer the mixture to a clean kitchen towel and roll it up tightly in the towel. Holding the towel over the sink and grasping one end in each hand, twist the towel to wring out as much liquid as possible.

Unwrap the well-squeezed potato-onion mixture and place it in a large bowl. Add the egg, scallions, flour, and salt and mix well.

**To cook the pancakes:** Line a rimmed baking sheet or large platter with paper towels. In a large skillet, heat the ½ cup vegetable oil over medium-high heat until it shimmers. To form a pancake, scoop ¼ cup of the batter into the oil and press down on it with the bottom of the measuring cup to form a round cake about 3½ inches in diameter and ⅓ to ½ inch thick. Repeat to form more pancakes, being careful not to crowd them. Cook, turning once, until golden brown on both sides and cooked through, 3 to 4 minutes on each side. Using a slotted spatula, transfer the pancakes to the towel-lined baking sheet, and tent loosely with aluminum foil to keep warm while you cook the remaining batter the same way.

Transfer the pancakes to a warmed platter and serve hot. Pass the applesauce and sour cream at the table.

# Mom's Brisket

"Well…I added the ketchup, but the rest is basically Mom's. I've been eating this all my life, and it's never once been dry or tough. The trick is, you cook it, cool it, slice it, and then reheat it in its own gravy when it's time to eat. For a big group, it's a dream come true."

**SERVES 6 TO 8**

**ONION SAUCE**

¼ cup canola oil

4 cups thinly sliced onions (about 2 large onions)

2 cups sliced, peeled carrots (about 2 medium carrots sliced ¼ inch thick)

4 cloves garlic, chopped

2 bay leaves

1 teaspoon kosher salt

1 teaspoon freshly ground black pepper

1 teaspoon onion powder

1 teaspoon garlic powder

1 cup chicken or beef broth

1 cup ketchup

½ cup whole-grain mustard

2 envelopes Lipton's onion soup mix

⅓ cup Worcestershire sauce

¼ cup minced fresh flat-leaf parsley

1 brisket (preferably first cut), about 6 pounds, with a good amount of marbling

About 2 cups beef broth

2 tablespoons chopped fresh flat-leaf parsley

Preheat the oven to 400°F.

**For the onion sauce:** In a large sauté pan, heat the canola oil over medium heat until it shimmers. Add the onions and cook, stirring occasionally, until soft and golden brown, 10 to 12 minutes. Add the carrots and cook, stirring occasionally, for 4 minutes, then add the garlic and bay leaves and cook for 2 minutes longer. Season with the salt, pepper, onion powder, and garlic powder and stir until fragrant, about 1 minute. Pour in the 1 cup broth and mix well. Remove from the heat and whisk in the ketchup, mustard, onion soup mix, and Worcestershire sauce until fully incorporated.

**For the brisket:** Place the meat, fat side up, in a roasting pan or baking dish just large enough to accommodate it. Pour the onion sauce over the brisket and cover the pan tightly with aluminum foil. Place in the oven and cook for 2 hours. Reduce the oven temperature to 350°F and continue to cook for 2½ hours longer. Remove from the oven and reduce the oven temperature to 325°F. Remove the foil, spoon some of the sauce in the pan over the brisket, and return the pan to the oven, uncovered. Cook, basting the brisket every 10 minutes or so with the sauce, until the meat is tender when pierced with a fork, about 30 minutes longer. Remove from the oven and let the brisket cool to room temperature in the pan.

**To serve:** Preheat the oven to 325°F. Transfer the cooled brisket to a cutting board and slice it against the grain as thinly as possible. If the sauce is very thick, dilute it with as much of the 2 cups broth as needed to achieve the consistency of a thick gravy. Slip the meat slices into the sauce, and cover the pan with aluminum foil. Reheat the brisket in the oven until warmed through, about 30 minutes.

Transfer the meat slices to a warmed deep platter, spoon the sauce over the slices, and scatter the parsley over the top. Serve right away.

# Zeppole

**MAKES ABOUT 20 PASTRIES;
SERVES 6 TO 8**

**DOUGH**

4 tablespoons butter

¼ cup granulated sugar

½ teaspoon salt

1 cup water

1 cup all-purpose flour

4 large eggs

Olive oil or canola oil for deep-frying

Ground cinnamon and granulated or
   confectioners' sugar for dusting

**For the dough:** In a small saucepan, combine the butter, granulated sugar, salt, and water over medium-high heat and bring to a boil, stirring with a wooden spoon until the sugar dissolves. Stir in the flour all at once with the spoon and immediately reduce the heat to the lowest setting. Continue to stir until the dough comes together in a ball and is shiny, 2 to 3 minutes.

Transfer the dough to a stand mixer fitted with the paddle attachment and let cool to room temperature. With the mixer on low speed, add the eggs one at a time, mixing after each addition until fully incorporated. Once all of the eggs have been added and the dough is thick, remove the bowl from the mixer stand, cover the bowl with plastic wrap, and let the dough rest for 10 minutes.

**To deep-fry the pastries:** Pour the oil to a depth of 2 inches into a large, heavy-bottomed saucepan, place over medium-high heat, and heat to 350°F. Line a large plate with several layers of paper towels.

Working in batches, and using a small ice-cream scoop or 2 spoons, scoop rounded tablespoons of the dough into the hot oil and fry the pastries, turning them occasionally with a slotted spoon, until golden brown, about 4 minutes. Using the slotted spoon, transfer the pastries to the towel-lined plate to drain. Repeat with the remaining dough.

Dust the hot pastries with cinnamon and sugar and serve immediately.

**MICHELLE'S TIPS:** You can gild the lily by serving *zeppole* with chocolate sauce or *dulce de leche,* or use a pastry bag to fill them with lemon curd.

Taste one of your first few *zeppole* to gauge the oil temperature. If it's greasy, the oil isn't hot enough; if it's raw inside, the oil is too hot (and nothing's worse than "lead *zeppole*"!).

"I've always been a sucker for anything fried and sweet, especially in the doughnut family. *Zeppole* are Italy's most famous fried-dough treat, and I got this recipe from an old Jewish woman in Venice."

## TAKASHI YAGIHASHI
# NEW YEAR'S EVE PARTY

"In Japan, there's no going out and partying on New Year's Eve," says Takashi. "It's a time to stay home and be with your family. But the days that follow are all about visiting and socializing, and, of course, eating up a storm." His elegant New Year's Eve menu features a mouthwatering mix of hot and cold Japanese dishes that are easy to make at home.

# Shrimp Cocktail

"People love shrimp at a party. I like to fix them simply and then add some fun and flavor with the sauces, so I came up with three easy but very tasty ones to serve on the side."

**SERVES 8**

### YUZU TARTAR SAUCE

6 tablespoons mayonnaise

¼ cup minced shallots

4 teaspoons capers, minced

2 tablespoons minced cornichons or sour pickles

2 tablespoons minced pickled ginger

2 teaspoons bottled yuzu juice or fresh lime juice

2 tablespoons chopped fresh dill

### ASIAN COCKTAIL SAUCE

¾ cup ketchup

¼ cup wasabi paste

¼ cup chile bean sauce (preferably Japanese *tobanjan*)

1 tablespoon bottled yuzu juice or fresh lime juice

### SWEET ONION SAUCE

2 cloves garlic

½ onion, coarsely chopped

6 tablespoons rice vinegar

¼ cup Asian sesame oil

¼ cup Japanese soy sauce

2 tablespoons sugar

¼ teaspoon freshly ground black pepper

Crushed ice

2 cups microgreens such as mizuna, arugula, or cilantro

4 large cherry tomatoes, quartered, or 8 small cherry tomatoes, halved

24 jumbo (U10) shrimp, boiled, peeled with tail segments attached, and deveined, then chilled

2 lemons, each cut into 6 wedges

**For the yuzu tartar sauce:** In a small bowl, whisk together all of the ingredients. You should have about 1½ cups. Use immediately, or cover and refrigerate for up to 2 days.

**For the Asian cocktail sauce:** In a small bowl, whisk together all of the ingredients. You should have about 1½ cups. Use immediately, or cover and refrigerate for up to 2 days.

**For the sweet onion sauce:** In a small blender, combine all of the ingredients and process until smooth. You should have about 1½ cups. Use immediately, or cover and refrigerate for up to 3 days.

Fill three 12-ounce martini glasses three-fourths full with crushed ice. Set each glass in the middle of a large plate. Scatter the microgreens evenly over the ice in each glass, and sprinkle the tomato pieces over the greens. Hang 8 shrimp off of the rim of each glass, hooking their curled ends over the lip (with the tails pointing downward). Try to space the shrimp evenly around the circumference of each glass. Arrange 3 small dipping bowls on the plate around the base of each glass. For each glass, fill 1 bowl with the yuzu tartar sauce, another with the Asian cocktail sauce, and the third bowl with the sweet onion sauce. Place 2 lemon wedges near the dipping bowls on each plate. Serve immediately

# **Crispy Tacos** with Soy-Caramel Braised Pork

"Braised pork belly is one of our signature dishes at Takashi. This version, made with pork shoulder, uses the same two-step process: first you simmer the meat to take away some of the fat and the 'porkiness,' and then you braise it to put flavor back in. Finally, you chill and slice the pork and caramelize it under the broiler. It's worth the effort, especially when you taste it in a crispy taco shell."

### MAKES 8 TACOS; SERVES 8

1¼ pounds boneless pork shoulder, in one piece

2 tablespoons vegetable oil

8 cups cold water

1 cup sake

Two 2-inch pieces fresh ginger, peeled and smashed with a chef's knife

### BRAISING LIQUID

3 cups cold water

2 cups Japanese soy sauce

1½ cups sugar

2 pieces star anise

1 teaspoon black peppercorns

2 cinnamon sticks

2-inch piece fresh ginger, peeled and smashed with a chef's knife

### PICKLED CUCUMBERS

½ to ¾ English cucumber

1 cup rice vinegar

½ cup mirin

1½ teaspoons soy sauce

2 tablespoons sugar

Pinch of red pepper flakes

### MUSTARD SAUCE

4 teaspoons mustard powder

4 teaspoons water

### HOISIN GLAZE

2 cups reserved braising liquid

½ cup hoisin sauce

4 teaspoons cornstarch

4 teaspoons water

Nonstick cooking spray

8 store-bought crispy taco shells

½ head iceberg lettuce, cored and finely julienned (about 2 cups)

16 fresh cilantro sprigs

1 teaspoon black sesame seeds

Cut the pork shoulder in half, then trim each half into a piece 10 inches long by 3 inches wide by 2 inches thick. In a large sauté pan, heat the vegetable oil over high heat. Add 1 pork piece and sear it on all 4 sides until golden brown, 2 to 3 minutes on each side. Transfer to a large saucepan. Sear the remaining piece of pork the same way and add it to the saucepan.

Add the water to the saucepan. It should just cover the meat. Add the sake and ginger, place over high heat, and bring to a boil. Reduce the heat to a gentle simmer and cook for 45 minutes.

While the pork is simmering, prepare the braising liquid: In a large saucepan, combine the water, soy sauce, sugar, star anise, peppercorns, cinnamon sticks, and ginger and bring to a boil over medium-high heat, stirring to dissolve the sugar. Remove from the heat and reserve.

When the pork is ready, drain it and discard the liquid. Add the pork pieces to the reserved braising liquid and place over high heat. Bring to a boil, reduce the heat to a gentle simmer, cover, and cook over low heat until the pork is very tender when pierced with a fork, about 45 minutes. Remove from the heat and let the pork cool to room temperature in the braising liquid.

Transfer the cooled pork to a plate, cover, and refrigerate until well chilled, about 1 hour. Strain the cooking liquid through a fine-mesh sieve. Measure 2 cups of the liquid to use for the hoisin glaze and set aside. Discard the remaining braising liquid.

While the pork is cooking, make the pickled cucumber slices and the mustard sauce: For the cucumber slices, using a mandoline, very thinly slice the cucumber to yield 32 slices. Place the slices in a heatproof bowl. In a small saucepan, combine the vinegar, mirin, soy sauce, sugar, and pepper flakes and bring to a boil over high heat, stirring to dissolve the sugar. Remove from the heat, pour over the cucumber slices, and let cool to room temperature. Cover and refrigerate for at least 2 hours before serving. The pickled slices will keep for up to 1 week.

**To make the mustard sauce:** In a small bowl, stir together the mustard powder and water and set aside.

**To make the hoisin glaze:** In a small saucepan, combine the braising liquid and hoisin sauce over high heat and bring to a boil. Meanwhile, in a small bowl, stir together the cornstarch and water until smooth. When the braising mixture begins to boil, whisk in the cornstarch mixture and cook briefly, just until the glaze begins to thicken. It should have the consistency of syrup. Remove from the heat and set aside.

Preheat the broiler. Line a rimmed baking sheet with aluminum foil and spray the foil with cooking spray.

Cut each chilled pork piece crosswise into 8 equal slices. Arrange the 16 pork slices, not overlapping, on the prepared baking sheet. Brush the pork

generously with the some of the hoisin glaze. Place under the broiler and broil until the meat is caramelized and warmed through, 3 to 4 minutes, watching closely to make sure the pork doesn't burn. Remove the meat from the oven, turn off the broiler, and warm the taco shells briefly in the residual oven heat.

**To build the tacos:** For each taco, place ¼ cup lettuce in the bottom of a warmed taco shell. Lay 2 pork slices the length of the shell, overlapping them

if necessary. Top with 4 pickled cucumber slices and a drizzle of the remaining hoisin glaze. Add a few drops of the mustard sauce, then finish with 2 cilantro sprigs and a sprinkle of black sesame seeds. Repeat with the remaining ingredients and taco shells.

"Yakitori means a party, because you either go out to eat it with a group or you make it for a crowd at home. I like to serve a mix of chicken, beef, shrimp, and vegetable skewers all through the evening."

# Yakitori

**MAKES 32 SKEWERS; SERVES 8**

### YAKITORI SAUCE

2 cups soy sauce

⅓ cup sake

⅓ cup water

¼ cup fresh lemon juice

2 tablespoons Asian sesame oil

4 teaspoons ginger juice

2 cups sugar

1 teaspoon red pepper flakes

### CHICKEN YAKITORI

1 pound boneless, skinless chicken breast or thigh meat, cut into twenty-four 1-inch pieces

4 scallions, including tender green parts, cut into 1-inch pieces

### BEEF YAKITORI

1 pound beef tenderloin, cut into twelve 1-inch cubes

1 yellow onion, cut into 1-inch pieces

### SHRIMP YAKITORI

16 extra-large (U16) shrimp, peeled, deveined, and each cut crosswise into 3 pieces

4 asparagus spears (not pencil thin), ends trimmed and each spear cut into four 1-inch pieces

### VEGETABLE YAKITORI

6 large shiitake mushrooms, each 2 to 3 inches in diameter, stemmed and quartered, or 12 smaller mushroom caps, stemmed and halved

4 asparagus spears (not pencil thin), ends trimmed and each spear cut into four 1-inch pieces

1 red bell pepper, seeded and cut into sixteen 1-inch squares

Vegetable oil for the grill rack or pan

Soak 32 bamboo skewers, each 6 inches long, in water to cover for at least 30 minutes.

**For the yakitori sauce**: In a saucepan, combine the soy sauce, sake, water, lemon juice, sesame oil, ginger juice, and sugar over high heat and bring to a boil, stirring until the sugar dissolves. Add the pepper flakes, remove from the heat, and reserve.

**For the chicken yakitori:** Thread a piece of chicken onto a bamboo skewer. Push it down the length of the skewer, leaving 1 inch of wood exposed at the end for a handle. Next, add a piece or two of scallion (use 2 pieces if the pieces are thin), add another piece of chicken, more scallion, and finally a third piece of chicken (the skewer should have 3 pieces of chicken and 2 pieces of scallion). Repeat with the remaining ingredients to build 8 skewers total. Set aside.

**For the beef yakitori:** Thread a piece of beef onto a bamboo skewer. Push it down the length of the skewer, leaving 1 inch of wood exposed at the end for a handle. Next, add a piece of onion, add another piece of beef, another piece of onion, and finally a third piece of beef (the skewer should have 3 pieces of beef and 2 pieces of onion). Repeat with the remaining ingredients to build 8 skewers total. Set aside.

**For the shrimp yakitori:** Thread 2 shrimp pieces onto a bamboo skewer. Push them down the length of the skewer, leaving 1 inch of wood exposed at the end for a handle. Next, add a piece of asparagus, add 2 more shrimp pieces, another piece of asparagus, and finally 2 more shrimp pieces (the skewer should have 6 shrimp pieces and 2 pieces of asparagus). Repeat with the remaining ingredients to build 8 skewers total. Set aside.

**For the vegetable yakitori:** Thread 1 mushroom piece onto a bamboo skewer. Push it down the length of the skewer, leaving 1 inch of wood exposed at the end for a handle. Next, add an asparagus piece, then a bell pepper piece, another mushroom piece, another asparagus piece, another bell pepper piece, and finally a mushroom piece (the skewer should have 3 mushroom pieces and 2 pieces each asparagus and bell pepper). Repeat with the remaining ingredients to build 8 skewers total. Set aside.

Preheat a gas grill to medium, light a fire in a charcoal grill and let it burn just until the coals are covered with gray ash and medium-hot, or preheat a stove-top grill pan over medium heat.

Lightly oil the grill rack or the grill pan. Set 8 to 12 skewers on the rack or pan, making sure the exposed part of each skewer hangs over the edge (so it won't burn). Cook for 2 minutes, then turn the skewers. Using a pastry brush, coat each skewer generously with some of the yakitori sauce and cook for 3 minutes. Flip the yakitori again, brush with more sauce, and cook for 3 minutes more. Flip the yakitori again, brush with more sauce, and grill until the skewered ingredients are cooked through and the sauce is caramelized, about 2 minutes more. Repeat with the remaining skewers.

Line up the grilled yakitori on a platter and serve right away.

# Toshikoshi Soba

**SERVES 8**

**DASHI BROTH**

3 large pieces dried *kombu* (kelp), each 10 by 4 inches, gently wiped with a damp towel

3 quarts plus 1½ cups water

4½ cups packed *katsuobushi* (dried bonito flakes)

1 cup Japanese soy sauce

1 cup mirin

8 pieces *abura-age* (fried tofu puffs), about 2 ounces total weight

1 cup halved, stemmed enoki mushrooms

24 snow peas, trimmed

1¾ pounds dried soba noodles

4 scallions, including tender green parts, thinly sliced on the diagonal

6 ounces *kamaboko* (fish cake), cut into twenty-four ¼-inch-thick slices

Leaves from 4 fresh mitsuba or chervil sprigs, chopped

Kosher salt

*Ichimi togarashi* (Japanese red pepper flakes), optional

**For the dashi:** In a large stockpot, combine the *kombu* and water and let soak at room temperature for at least 20 minutes. (You can soak as long as overnight, which will allow the *kombu* to release more flavor.) Place over high heat and bring to a boil. Remove and discard the *kombu* and reduce the heat so the liquid is at a simmer. Add the *katsuobushi* and gently mix into the liquid; do not stir vigorously. Simmer gently for 10 minutes longer.

Strain through a fine-mesh sieve and discard the contents of the sieve. You should have about 3 quarts broth. Measure 2½ quarts (10 cups) for the soba broth and reserve the remainder for another use.

**For the soba broth:** Rinse the stockpot, add the 2½ quarts dashi, the soy sauce, and the mirin and bring to a boil over high heat. Reduce the heat to medium and simmer for 2 minutes. Add the *abura-age* and the enoki, cover, and remove from the heat. Keep warm until ready to serve.

**To assemble the dish:** Prepare an ice bath. Bring a large pot three-fourths full of salted water to a boil over high heat. Add the peas and cook for 1 minute. Using a skimmer, transfer the peas to the ice bath to halt the cooking, then drain. Add the noodles to the boiling water and stir with a fork or chopsticks to make sure they don't stick together. Cook until al dente, 4 to 5 minutes, then drain.

Divide the noodles among 8 warmed bowls. Ladle 1¼ cups of the soba broth into each bowl, and divide the *aburage-age,* enoki mushrooms, peas, scallions, *kamaboko,* and mitsuba evenly among the bowls. Sprinkle each serving with a pinch of salt and with a pinch of *ichimi togarashi,* if using. Serve at once.

"Eating *toshikoshi* (year-end) soba on New Year's Eve is a Japanese national tradition. The buckwheat noodles are believed to cleanse your body for the year ahead. They're also a perfect light dish to enjoy at midnight."

"Dorayaki, pancake sandwiches filled with red bean paste, are a popular Japanese snack with tea. To turn them into a party dessert, I add candied walnuts and top them with ice cream and honey. They're like miniature pancake sundaes."

# Dorayaki Pancakes

**SERVES 8**

**CANDIED WALNUTS**

½ cup walnuts

Nonstick cooking spray

½ cup sugar

¼ cup water

2 teaspoons light corn syrup

**SIMPLE SYRUP**

6 tablespoons sugar

6 tablespoons water

**PANCAKE BATTER**

4 large eggs

1 cup all-purpose flour

1 cup cake flour

1 cup sugar

1 teaspoon baking powder

½ to 1 cup water

2 tablespoons honey

Nonstick cooking spray

¾ cup canned sweet red bean paste

1 pint vanilla ice cream

Honey for serving

**For the candied walnuts:** Preheat the oven to 350°F.

Spread the walnuts on a small rimmed baking sheet and place in the oven until they take on color and are fragrant, 10 to 15 minutes. Remove from the oven and let cool, then chop.

Place an 8-inch sheet of parchment paper on a work surface and spray with cooking spray. In an 8-inch sauté pan, combine the sugar, water, and corn syrup over medium-high heat and cook, without stirring, until the mixture turns a medium amber, 8 to 10 minutes. Add the walnuts, stir to coat with the caramel, and remove from the heat. Pour the nut mixture onto the prepared parchment, spread evenly with a heat-resistant rubber spatula, and let cool completely. Transfer to a cutting board and finely chop. The candied walnuts may be stored in an airtight container at room temperature for up to 3 days.

**For the simple syrup:** In a heavy-bottomed saucepan, combine the sugar and water over medium heat and bring to a boil, stirring occasionally. Continue to boil, stirring occasionally, until the sugar is dissolved, about 2 minutes. Remove from the heat and let cool to room temperature. You should have about ½ cup. Set aside.

**For the pancake batter:** In a large bowl, whisk the eggs until blended. Sift together both flours, the sugar, and the baking powder into the bowl with the eggs. Add ½ cup of the water and the honey and stir just until the ingredients are evenly combined. The batter should be thick and pourable and have the consistency of a milk shake. If it is too thick, stir in up to ½ cup more water.

Spray a large nonstick sauté pan with nonstick spray and place over medium heat. When the pan is hot, pour in the batter to form 3-inch pancakes, using about 3 tablespoons batter for each pancake and being careful not to crowd the pan. Cook until browned on the first side, 2 to 3 minutes, then flip and cook until browned on the second side, 2 to 3 minutes longer. Using a spatula, transfer the pancakes to a large plate. Wipe out the pan, spray it again with cooking spray, and repeat with the remaining batter. You should have 16 pancakes total. (The pancakes may be made up to 24 hours in advance. Let cool to room temperature, wrap with plastic wrap, and refrigerate. To rewarm, place in a microwave for 30 to 45 seconds.)

**To assemble:** Lay the 16 warm pancakes, with the sides that were browned first face down, on a work surface. Brush each pancake with about 1½ teaspoons of the simple syrup. Spread 1½ tablespoons of the red bean paste on each of 8 of the pancakes, leaving a ¼-inch border around the edge uncovered (this is the bottom of the pancake sandwich). Sprinkle the candied walnuts evenly over the bean paste on each pancake. Top with a second pancake, simple syrup side down, to form a sandwich.

Transfer the pancake sandwiches to individual plates. Top each serving with a scoop of ice cream and with a drizzle of honey, if desired. Serve right away

# Index

# Acknowledgments

A lively parade of talented people had a hand in shaping this book.

We thank Chairman, President and Chief Executive Officer, Macy's, Inc., Terry Lundgren for writing the foreword. Both he and Martine Reardon, Executive Vice President of Marketing and Advertising, lent invaluable support to the project.

And of course, many thanks to The Macy's Culinary Council—Rick Bayless, Michelle Bernstein, Cat Cora, Tom Douglas, Todd English, Marc Forgione, Emeril Lagasse, Wolfgang Puck, Marcus Samuelsson, Tim Scott, Nancy Silverton, Ming Tsai, and Takashi Yagihashi—for contributing their recipes and ideas, for making time for our photo shoots in New York and Los Angeles, and for all they do for Macy's throughout the year. Thanks also to Warren Wolf, the man who cooked up the Council in the first place, for his unfailing goodwill.

Big thanks to Elizabeth Brown for overseeing the complex recipe-testing process and the development of the Thanksgiving Basics chapter with her usual grace, accuracy, patience, and razor wit.

Maren Caruso, a true artist and a delightful creative partner, shot the mouthwatering food photography throughout the book. We thank her and her team—assistants Shawn Franzen, Austin Goldin, and Harrison Budd—as well as retoucher Ian Stout for their talent and their commitment. Style Director George Dolese conceived a look and palette for each menu and gave every photo the light-handed touch of storytelling and spontaneity he is renowned for, working in collaboration with masterful co-food stylist Elisabet der Nederlanden. Thanks also to Leigh Noe for sourcing the perfect props to bring the parties on these pages to life, and to Lisa and Sandy Wood for prop assistance and hand modeling. At Macy's Northwest, Megan Mahoney and Stephanie Morgan were indispensable in helping us source props, as well.

Cheers and thanks to Quentin Bacon for shooting the chef portraits in three cities, and to his assistant, Lauren Volo. David Sommers produced our New York chef shoot with the help of fashion stylist Fred Bernstein, prop stylist Natasha Louise King, and hair and makeup artist Paul Fields.

Thank you Kent Miller for the supplemental portrait photography in the parade section of the book.

Eugene Flynn of Amanda's Restaurant, thank you for your recipes, your time, and your love of the parade.

We thank our copy editor Sharon Silva for meeting the ever-changing deadlines and complexities of this project with patience, intelligence, accuracy, and drollness; Ellen Wheat for smart and speedy editorial consultation and proofreading; Hal Belmont of Overseas Printing Corporation for his support and great work; and indexer Ken DellaPenta.

It's a joy to work with the Macy's team. We thank Amy Kule, Group Vice President, Macy's Parade and Entertainment Group. Her vision and love of the parade and the people who make it happen inspired this book two years ago, and she has been its enthusiastic champion ever since. We also thank Robin Hall, Senior Vice President, Macy's Parade and Entertainment Group, for his commitment to the project. We're grateful to Kelly Lainsbury for shepherding this book every step of the way. Her make-it-happen attitude, problem-solving ingenuity, sense of humor under pressure, and juggling skills are unrivaled. We thank Stacy Rosenthal, Director, Macy's Special Events for Home, for her excitement and help throughout the process. Scott Byers, Macy's historian, helped source archival photography and information, ably assisted by Brandi Reidburn. Orlando Veras provided invaluable input and fact-checking. We thank the lead parade creative and production team—Bill Schermerhorn, Susan Babb, John Piper, and Jordan Dabby—for their helpful feedback as well. Thanks also to Manager, Macy's Special Events for Home, Jodi Riddick, and to Tiffani McCallon for organizational and editorial support. We thank Helane Blumfield, John Murphy, and Denton Warne, for their creative vision and collaborative spirit.

Every year, the thousands of men, women, and kids who make up the Macy's Thanksgiving Day Parade volunteers and staff come together to spend their Thanksgiving helping the world start the holiday season with a sense of tradition and a spirit of magic and wonder. That's something we can all be thankful for, and this book is dedicated to them.

Catherine Jacobes and Steve Siegelman
The Book Kitchen

Produced by The Book Kitchen, San Francisco, for Macy's.

www.bookkitchen.com

Art direction/design: **Catherine Jacobes**

Text/editorial direction: **Steve Siegelman**

Food photography: **Maren Caruso**

Food photography assistance: **Shawn Franzen, Austin Goldin, Harrison Budd**

Portrait photography: **Quentin Bacon**

Portrait photography assistance: **Lauren Volo**

Style direction: **George Dolese**

Food stylists: **George Dolese** and **Elisabet der Nederlanden**

Prop stylist: **Leigh Noe**

Styling assistance: **Lisa Wood** and **Sandy Wood**

NY portrait fashion stylist: **Fred Bernstein**

NY portrait prop stylist: **Natasha Louise King**

Additional portrait photography: **Kent Miller**

Recipe tester: **Elizabeth Brown**

Copy editor: **Sharon Silva**

Proofreader and editorial consultant: **Ellen Wheat**

Indexer: **Ken DellaPenta**

Digital imaging for parade and chef images: **Ian Stout**

ISBN: 978-09779890-5-8
First printing, 2011
10.9.8.7.6.5.4.3.2.1

Manufactured in China by Overseas Printing Corporation